Daniel Gatty is a barrister at Gatehouse Chambers. He specialises in disputes about property, especially real property and commercial landlord and tenant and also mortgages and secured lending. In addition to practising at the Bar, he is an experienced mediator and sits as a part-time Judge of the First-tier Tribunal (Property Chamber, Land Registration).

A Practical Guide to Rights Over Airspace and Subsoil
Second Edition

A Practical Guide to Rights Over Airspace and Subsoil
Second Edition

Daniel Gatty

BA (Econ) Hons, Dip Law

Barrister, Gatehouse Chambers, London

Judge of the First-tier Tribunal (Property Chamber)

Law Brief Publishing

© Daniel Gatty

All rights reserved. No part of this publication may be reproduced, stored in a retrieval system, or transmitted, in any form or by any means, electronic, mechanical, photocopying, recording or otherwise, without the prior permission of the publisher.

Excerpts from judgments and statutes are Crown copyright. Any Crown Copyright material is reproduced with the permission of the Controller of OPSI and the King's Printer for Scotland. Some quotations may be licensed under the terms of the Open Government Licence (http://www.nationalarchives.gov.uk/doc/open-government-licence/version/3).

Cover image © iStockphoto.com/georgeclerk

The information in this book was believed to be correct at the time of writing. All content is for information purposes only and is not intended as legal advice. No liability is accepted by either the publisher or author for any errors or omissions (whether negligent or not) that it may contain. Professional advice should always be obtained before applying any information to particular circumstances.

Published 2023 by Law Brief Publishing, an imprint of Law Brief Publishing Ltd
30 The Parks
Minehead
Somerset
TA24 8BT

www.lawbriefpublishing.com

Paperback: 978-1-916698-23-9

PREFACE TO FIRST EDITION

"If you have built castles in the air, your work need not be lost; that is where they should be. Now put the foundations under them."
– Henry David Thoreau

When I was approached to write this book I hesitated, wondering whether a text confined to legal rights over airspace and subsoil would prove of interest, let alone use, to anyone at all. On reflection, though, I came to realise that a concise book pulling together various different legal considerations that may affect a development below ground level or above an existing building ought to be of real value in these days of housing shortage. Or so I hope. This book is intended as a practical guide and not a work of academic scholarship. Some of the topics it covers are too extensive for comprehensive analysis in a book this size but even in those areas I have sought to point the reader in the right direction.

I would like to express my gratitude to my former pupil, now colleague, Priya Gopal, for checking the first proofs and to my publishers, Law Brief Publishing, for suggesting that I write the book and supporting me while I did so. Most of all I would like to thank my wife and children for not complaining too much when I took absence from family life to write it.

I have endeavoured to state the law as at 31 August 2019.

Daniel Gatty
Hardwicke
New Square
Lincoln's Inn
London
October 2019

PREFACE TO SECOND EDITION

When I wrote the preface to the first edition of this book four years ago I cautiously suggested that a book discussing the legal considerations that affect a development below ground level or above an existing building might be useful in a time of housing shortage. Since then, the housing shortage in the U.K. has worsened and so I hope that this second edition may prove useful too.

I have endeavoured to state the law as at 31 July 2023.

Daniel Gatty
Gatehouse Chambers
Gray's Inn
London
September 2023

TABLE OF CASES

Abbahall Ltd v Smee [2003] 1 WLR 1472 ... 8

Albion Residential Ltd v Albion Riverside Residents RTM Company Ltd [2014] UKUT 0006 (LC) ... 57

Aldford House Freehold Ltd v Grosvenor (Mayfair) Estate [2019] EWCA Civ 1848, [2020] Ch 270 ... 52, 59

Ali v Lane [2006] EWCA Civ 1532 ... 16

Allen v Greenwood [1980] Ch 119 ... 47

Anchor Brewhouse Developments Ltd v Berkley House (Docklands Developments) Ltd [1987] 2 EGLR 173 ... 5

Anglo International Upholland Ltd v Wainwright and persons unknown (2023, Unrep.) ... 5

Apache North Sea Ltd v Euroil Exploration Ltd [2020] EWCA Civ 1397 ... 15

Ashton v Stock (1877) 6 Ch D 719 ... 15

ARC Aggregates Ltd v Branston Properties Ltd [2020] EWHC 1976 (Ch), [2021] 2 P & CR 1 ... 66, 73

Attorney-General v Morgan [1891] 1 Ch 432 ... 3

Barney v BP Truckstops [1995] NPC 5 ... 44

Bass v Gregory (1890) 25 QBD 481 ... 45-46

Beaumont Business Centres v Florala Properties [2020] EWHC 550 (Ch) ... 48

Bellamy v Debenham [1891] 1 Ch 412 ... 32

Bernstein of Leigh v Skyviews & General [1978] QB 479 ... 4-5

Bocardo SA v Star Energy UK Onshore Ltd [2010] UKSC 35 ... 1, 2-3, 5, 78

Bockenfield Aerodrome Ltd v Clarehugh [2021] EWHC 848 (Ch), [2022] 1 P & CR 17 ... 46

Bond v Nottingham Corporation [1940] Ch 429 ... 41

Bonomi v Backhouse (1858) El Bl & El 622 ... 39

Bryant v Lefever (1879) 4 CPD 172 ... 45

Build Hollywood Ltd v London Borough of Hackney [2022] EWHC 2806 (Admin)...97

Bury v Pope (1586) Croke, Elizabeth 118 ... 1

Butterknowle Colliery Co v Bishop Auckland Industrial Co-operative Co [1906] AC 305 ... 67, 68

Cable v Bryant [1908] 1 Ch 259 ... 46

Cherry Tree Investments v Landmain [2012] EWCA Civ 736 ... 17

Coleman v Ibstock Brick [2008] EWCA Civ 73 ... 63

Colls v Home and Colonial Stores Ltd [1904] AC1 79 ... 47

Consensus Business Group (Ground Rents) v Palgrave Gardens Freehold Co Ltd [2020] EWHC 920 (Ch), [2020] 2 P & CR 13 ... 57

Coopind (UK) Ltd v Walton Commercial Group Ltd [1989] 1 EGLR 241 ... 43

Corbett v Hill (1869-70) LR 9 Eq 671 ... 11

Coventry v Lawrence [2014] UKSC 13, [2014] AC 822 ... 7, 69

Cunliffe v Whalley (1851) 13 Beav 411 ... 13

Dalton v Angus & Co (1881) 6 App Cas 740 ... 38, 41

Dartmouth Court Blackheath Ltd v Berisworth Ltd [2008] EWHC 350 (Ch), [2008] 2 P & CR 3 ... 58, 60, 95

Davies v Yadegar (1990) 22 HLR 232 ... 19, 20-21, 23

Delgable Ltd v Perinpanathan [2005] EWCA Civ 1724 ... 19

Devonshire Reid Properties v Trenaman [1997] 1 EGLR 45 ... 90

Donovan v Rana [2014] EWCA Civ 99, [2014] 1 P & CR 23 ... 43

Duke of Westminster v Guild [1985] 1 QB 688 ... 43

Eardley v Granville (1876) 3 Ch D 826 ... 70

Earl of Lonsdale v Attorney-General [1982] 1 WLR 887 ... 63

Eason v Wong [2017] EWHC 209 (Ch) ... 33-34

Fay v Prentice (1845) 1 CB 828 ... 5

Fearn v Board of Trustees of Tate Gallery [2023] UKSC 4, [2023] 2 WLR 339 ... 45

Field v Freehold Properties 250 Ltd [2020] EWHC 792 (Ch), [2020] Ch 665 ... 58

Finchley Electric Light Co v Finchley UDC [1903] 1 Ch 437 ... 14, 18

Foster v Lyons & Co. [1927] 1 Ch 219 ... 93

Francia Properties v Aristou [2017] L & TR 5 ... 90, 95-96

Gardner v Hodgson's Kingston Brewery Co Ltd [1901] 2 Ch. 198; [1903] A.C. 229...39

Gifford v Dent [1926] WN 336 ... 5

Glasgow Corpn v Farie (1888) 13 App Cas 657 ... 63, 65

Gorst v Knight [2018] EWHC 613 (Ch) ... 22, 23, 24

Grigsby v Melville [1974] 1 WLR 80 ... 9-10

H Waites Ltd v Hambledon Court Ltd [2014] EWHC 651 (Ch) ... 18, 19, 21, 92

Hannon v 169 Queen's Gate Ltd [2000] 1 EGLR 40 ... 89, 90, 92

Harris v Ryding (1839) 5 M & W 60 ... 68

Heath v Dane [1905] 2 Ch 86 ... 66

Hemphurst Ltd v Durrels House Ltd [2011] UKUT 6 (LC), [2011] L & TR 16 ... 56

Holbeck Hall Hotel Ltd v Scarborough Borough Council [2000] QB 836 ... 40

Humphries v Brogden (1850) 12 QB 739 ... 39, 68

Hunter v Canary Wharf Ltd [1997] AC 655, 709 ... 45

J A Pye (Oxford) Ltd v Graham [2002] UKHL 30; [2003] 1 AC 419 ... 83

Kelsen v Imperial Tobacco Co (of Great Britain and Ireland) Ltd [1957] 2 QB 334 ... 5, 17

Laiqat v Majid [2005] EWHC 1305 (QB) ... 5

Lawson v Hartley-Brown (1996) 71 P & CR 242, CA ... 91

Laybourn v Gridley [1892] 2 Ch 53 ... 10, 11, 31

Lejonvarn v Cromwell Mansions Management Company Ltd [2011] EWHC 3838 (Ch) ... 22

Lemaitre v Davis (1881) 19 Ch D 281 ... 41

Levet v Gas Light and Coke Co. [1919] 1 Ch 24 … 47

Linvale Investment Ltd v Walker [2016] 2 P & CR 12 … 37

LM Homes v Queen Court Freehold Company Ltd [2020] EWCA Civ 371, [2020] QB 890… 24, 53-57

LM Homes v Queen Court Freehold Company Ltd [2018] UKUT 367 (LC)…24

Lotus Ltd v British Soda Co. Ltd [1972] Ch 123 … 40

MBR Acres v Free the MBR Beagles [2021] EWHC 2996 (QB) … 5

Merie Bin Mahfouz Company (UK) Ltd v Barrie House (Freehold) Ltd [2014] UKUT 0390 (LC) … 55

Midland Railway Co. v Wright [1901] Ch 738 … 83

Midtown Ltd v City of London Real Property Co Ltd [2005] EWHC 33, [2005] 1 EGLR 65 … 48

Ough v King [1967] 1 WLR 1547 … 48

Pennock v Hodgson [2010] EWCA Civ 873 … 9, 16

Petra Investments Ltd v Jeffrey Rogers Plc [2000] L & TR 45 … 92

Pickering v Rudd (1815) 4 Campbell 219 … 4

Popplewell v Hodkinson (1868-69) LR 4 Ex 248 … 40

Port v Griffith [1938] 1 All ER 295 … 90

Pyer v Carter (1857) 1 Hurl & N 916 … 43

R (HCP (Hendon) Ltd) v Chief Land Registrar [2020] 1 WLR 4240 … 20, 28

Rains v Buxton (1880) 14 Ch D 537 … 83, 85

Ralph Kline Ltd v Metropolitan and County Holdings Ltd [2018] EWHC 64 (Ch) … 18, 21

Rance v Elvin (1985) 50 P & CR 9 … 42

Ravengate Estates Limited v Horizon Housing Group Limited [2007] EWCA Civ 1368 … 18

Ray v Fairway Motors (Barnstaple) Ltd (1969) 20 P & CR 261 … 39

Re London, Tilbury & Southend Ry and the Trustees of the Gower's Walk Schools (1889) 24 QBD 326 … 47-48

Rhone v Stephens [1994] 2 AC 310 … 8

Rosebery Ltd v Rocklee Ltd [2011] L & TR 21 … 21

Rowe v Grenfel (1824) Ry & M 396 … 65

Rugby Joint Water Board v Walters [1967] Ch 397 … 45

Scarfe v Adams [1981] 1 All ER 843 … 29

Shelfer v City of London Electric Lighting Company [1895] 1 Ch 287 … 6

Sitwell v Earl of Londesborough [1905] 1 Ch 460 … 67

Southwark LBC v Transport for London [2018] UKSC 63, [2020] AC 914 … 2, 12, 13

Sovmots Investments Ltd v Secretary of State for the Environment [1979] AC 144 … 8

Stadium Capital Holdings v St Marylebone Properties Co Plc [2009] EWHC 2942 … 85

Straudley Investments Ltd v Barpress Ltd [1987] 1 EGLR 69 … 17

Stroyan v Knowles (1861) 6 Hurl & N 454 … 39

Swan Housing Association v Gill [2012] EWHC 3129 (QB), [2013] 1 WLR 1253 … 81

Tehidy Minerals Ltd v Norman [1971] 2 QB 528 … 38

Timothy Taylor Ltd v Mayfair House Corp [2016] 4 WLR 100 … 91

Trenberth (John) Ltd v National Westminster Bank Ltd (1979) 39 P & CR 104 … 6

Truckell v Stock [1957] 1 WLR 161 … 10, 30

Tunbridge Wells Corpn v Baird [1896] AC 434 … 12

Turner v Wakefeld [2004] EWCA Civ 1725 … 30-31

Vectis Property Company Ltd v Cambrai Court Management Company Ltd [2022] UKUT 42 (LC) … 56, 90-92

Webb v Bird (1861) 10 CB (ns) 268) … 45

Wheeldon v Burrows (1879) 12 Ch D 31 … 37-38

Williams, Armstrong v Alter Domus Trustees (UK) Ltd [2023] EWHC 1820 (Ch) … 34

Williams v Usherwood (1983) 45 P & CR 235, CA … 85

Wynne-Finch v Natural Resources Body for Wales [2020] EWHC 1924 (Ch) ... 4, 65, 75, 84

Wynne-Finch v Natural Resources Body for Wales [2021] EWCA Civ 1473 ... 65, 75, 84

York House (Chelsea) Ltd v Thompson [2019] EWHC 2203 (Ch) ... 60

TABLE OF LEGISLATION

Air Navigation Act 1920 ... 4
Air Navigation Order 2016 ... 6, 7
Air Traffic Management and Unmanned Aircraft Act 2021 ... 6
Airports Act 1986 ... 7
Civil Aviation Act 1982 ... 4, 5-7
Civil Aviation Act 2012 ... 7
Coal Industry Act 1994 ... 3, 65
Coal Mining Subsidence Act 1991 ... 69
Commonhold and Leasehold Reform Act 2002 ... 56, 95-96
Data Protection Act 2018 ... 6
Electricity Act 1989 ... 44
Electronic Communications Code 2017 ... 44
Gas Act 1986 ... 7, 44
Highways Act 1835 ... 12
Highways Act 1980 ... 13, 14, 96-97
Infrastructure Act 2015 ... 78-79
Interpretation Act 1978 ... 72
Land Registration Act 1925 ... 73-74
Land Registration Act 2002 ... 28, 32, 37, 73-74, 81, 82
Land Registration Rules 2003 ... 27, 32, 74
Landlord and Tenant Act 1927 ... 89
Landlord and Tenant Act 1954 ... 59
Landlord and Tenant Act 1987 ... 58-60, 95
Law of Property (Miscellaneous Provisions) Act 1989 ... 44, 68
Law of Property Act 1922 ... 69, 70, 71, 72, 73
Law of Property Act 1925 ... 7-8, 35, 36, 37, 41, 42, 66, 74
Leasehold Reform Act 1967 ... 51, 57-58, 66

Leasehold Reform and Urban Development Act 1993 ... 24, 51-57, 58, 59, 66

Limitation Act 1980 ... 81

Metropolis Management Act 1855 ... 12

Mines (Working Facilities and Support) Act 1966 ... 68, 78-79

Party Wall etc Act 1996 ... 88, 93

Petroleum Act 1998 ... 3, 78

Prescription Act 1832 ... 38, 39, 46, 93

Public Health Act 1848 ... 12

Public Health Act 1875 ... 12

Quia Emptores 1290 ... 70

Real Property Limitation Act 1835 ... 83

Rights of Light Act 1959 ... 48-49

Rules of the Air Regulations 2015 ... 7

Statute Law (Repeals) Act 1969 ... 72

Transport Act 2000 ... 7

Water Industry Act 1991 ... 44

Water Resources Act 1991 ... 40, 44, 45

CONTENTS

Chapter One	Freehold Ownership of Airspace and Subsoil	1
	1.1 Introduction	1
	1.2 Subsoil	2
	1.3 Airspace	4
	1.4 Statutory regulation of flight through airspace	7
	1.5 Dealings with freehold interests in airspace or subsoil	7
	1.6 Highways	12
Chapter Two	Leasehold Ownership of Airspace and Subsoil	15
	2.1 Introduction	15
	2.2 Airspace	17
	2.3 Subsoil	22
	2.4 Summary	25
Chapter Three	Conveyancing and Land Registration	27
	3.1 Land Registration Requirements	27
	3.2 Conveyancing in Relation to Airspace or Subsoil Generally	29
	3.3 Conveyancing of Interests in Mines and Minerals	32
	3.4 Liens Over Airspace	33

Chapter Four	Easements Affecting Airspace and Subsoil	35
	4.1 Introduction	35
	4.2 Acquisition of Easements	36
	4.3 Easements of Support	39
	4.4 Pipes, Drains and Underground Water	42
	4.5 Rights of Air	45
	4.6 Rights of Light	46
	4.7 Conclusion	49
Chapter Five	Leasehold Enfranchisement and Statutory Rights of First Refusal	51
	5.1 Leasehold Enfranchisement	51
	5.2. Right of First Refusal Under Landlord and Tenant Act 1987	58
	5.3 Conclusion	61
Chapter Six	Mines, Minerals and Manorial Rights	63
	A. Mines and Minerals	63
	6.1 Introduction	63
	6.2 The Meaning of Mines and Minerals	63
	6.3 Ownership	65
	6.4 Mining Leases	67

	6.5 Mining's Effects on the Surface	67
	B. Manorial Rights	69
	6.6 Introduction	69
	6.7 A Little Bit of Legal History	69
	6.8 Manorial Rights to Mines and Minerals Today	72
	6.9 Summary	75
Chapter Seven	Fracking	77
	7.1 Introduction	77
	7.2 Property Rights Considerations	77
Chapter Eight	Adverse Possession	81
	8.1 Introduction	81
	8.2 Adverse Possession of Subsoil	83
	8.3 Adverse Possession of Airspace	84
Chapter Nine	Building Above and Below Existing Buildings	87
	9.1 Introduction	87
	9.2 Who Owns the Airspace? Who Owns the Roof?	87
	9.3 Who Owns the Subsoil?	88
	9.4 Developments by Lessees	88
	9.5 Landlords' Obligations Under Flat Leases	89

9.6 Letting Schemes	92
9.7 Lessees' Easements	92
9.8 Rights of Light	93
9.9 Party Wall Etc Act 1996	93
9.10 Landlord and Tenant Act 1987	95
9.11 Right to Manage	95
9.12 Effect on Service Charges	96
9.13. Highways	96
Index	99

CHAPTER ONE

FREEHOLD OWNERSHIP OF AIRSPACE AND SUBSOIL

1. Introduction

The questions of who owns the air above our heads and the earth beneath our feet affects modern life in many ways. It may impact on a basement development under an expensive house in Holland Park, fracking in Lancashire (should fracking be permitted in the future), a landlord's wish to add a new floor on top of a block of flats or a hobbyist's desire to fly a drone over his neighbour's back garden. Modern statutes will be relevant to many of the issues that arise in this context but the starting point remains the common law and its treatment of the vertical extent of landownership.

Legal legend has it that the owner of land owns everything above it up to the sky and below it down to the centre of the earth or, to put it theologically, up to heaven and down to hell. The origin of that legend is a Latin maxim, cuius est solum eius est usque ad coelum et ad inferos (or some version of it), which has been attributed to Accursius, a commentator on Roman law who lived in Bologna in the 13th century. A form of the maxim is to be found in English law reports as early as the 16th century, in *Bury v Pope* (1586) Croke, Elizabeth 118. It was discussed by Lord Coke in 'On Littleton' published in 1628 and has cropped up in law reports and textbooks regularly ever since.

The maxim is an oversimplification as legal maxims tend to be, but not without force even today. In *Bocardo SA v Star Energy UK Onshore Ltd* [2010] UKSC 35 Lord Hope, with whom the rest of the Court agreed, held that, "the brocard[1] still has value in English law as encapsulating, in simple language, a proposition of law which has commanded general acceptance".

Its general acceptance can be seen from Lord Briggs's judgment in the Supreme Court case of *Southwark LBC v Transport for London* [2018] UKSC 63, [2020] AC 914 where he observed by way of introductory background:

> "A basic feature of the conveyance or transfer of freehold land by reference to an identified surface area is that, unless the context or the language of the grant otherwise requires or provides (e g by a reservation of minerals), its effect is to vest in the transferee not only the surface of the ground, but the subsoil down (at least in theory) to the centre of the earth and the air space up (at least in theory) into the heavens. Viewed in the vertical plane, the transferee acquires ownership not only of the slice on the surface but of the whole of the space above it, and the ground below it."

2. Subsoil

Bocardo is the leading authority on freehold ownership of subsoil. In that case Star Energy had a government issued licence to search for oil in a reservoir of petroleum and natural gas beneath land in Surrey. Star Energy's predecessor had bored under Bocardo's land and laid pipelines between 800 feet and 2,800 feet beneath the surface without Bocardo's consent. The licence permitted the extraction of the gas and petroleum below the surface (which belonged to the Crown by statute) but if Bocardo owned the strata down to that depth, the licence did not authorise the laying of pipes in the strata which would therefore be a trespass. Star Energy argued that Bocardo's ownership of the land did not extend down to the depths at which the pipelines had been installed. That

---

[1] A term meaning Latin legal maxim

argument was rejected. Lord Walker distinguished between subsoil and airspace (as to the latter see below). So far as subsoil is concerned, he held that:

> "...the owner of the surface is the owner of the strata beneath it, including the minerals that are to be found there, unless there has been an alienation of it by a conveyance, at common law or by statute to someone else... There must obviously be some stopping point, as one reaches the point at which physical features such as pressure and temperature render the concept of the strata belonging to anybody so absurd as to be not worth arguing about."

The pipelines, however, were "far from being so deep as to reach the point of absurdity" and hence were a trespass into Bocardo's land.

While the Supreme Court recognised in *Bocardo* that there was a depth below which it could not be meaningfully said that a landowner's ownership extends, it can be seen that this depth is so far below the surface that it is difficult to conceive of anyone laying claim to the strata below it. In practice, therefore, freeholders do own the soil below the surface "ad inferos", i.e. as far down as could have any conceivable practical use.

To that general statement there will be exceptions where the subsoil or minerals within it belong to someone else as a result of a conveyance, statute or the common law. As far as mines and minerals go, all gold and silver in mines vests in the Crown by common law (specifically by Royal Prerogative); see *Attorney-General v Morgan* [1891] 1 Ch 432. Petroleum in its natural condition in strata vests in the Crown by s. 2 of the Petroleum Act 1998 (consolidating earlier legislation). Unworked coal and coal mines are vested in the Coal Authority by s. 7 of the Coal Industry Act 1994 (having previously been vested in the British Coal Corporation and before that the National Coal Board and before that the Coal Commission, the previous iterations of what is now the Coal Authority).

For a recent discussion of the effect of an early nineteenth century enclosure act which separated out mines and minerals from the surface – leaving the mines and minerals under common and waste land owned by the Lord of the Manor while allotting the surface of the common and waste land, see *Wynne-Finch v Natural Resources Body for Wales* [2020] EWHC 1924 (Ch).

3. Airspace

The invention of manned flight created obvious difficulties with the application of the cuius est solum eius est usque ad coelum maxim to an indefinitely high column of airspace. Over two hundred years ago, in *Pickering v Rudd* (1815) 4 Campbell 219, Lord Ellenborough LCJ was to be found discussing whether the maxim would render "an aeronaut … liable to an action of trespass …, at the suit of the occupier of every field over which his balloon passes in the course of his voyage". He thought not.

Statutes such as the Air Navigation Act 1920 and the Civil Aviation Act 1982 provided protection from actions in trespass or nuisance by reason of aircraft flight over property at a reasonable height above the ground but did not attempt to refine the common law as to the vertical extent of land ownership. That has been left to the courts. In *Bernstein of Leigh v Skyviews & General* [1978] QB 479 Griffiths J observed that to apply the maxim literally would lead to the absurdity that it would be a trespass for a satellite to pass over a suburban garden. He held that the balance between a landowner's right to enjoy his land and the general public's rights to use airspace was:

> ".. best struck … by restricting the rights of an owner in the air space above his land to such height as is necessary for the ordinary use and enjoyment of his land and the structures upon it, and declaring that above that height he has no greater rights in the air space than any other member of the public".

Bernstein has been cited approvingly in various subsequent cases, including in the Supreme Court in *Bocardo*, and must be taken to be a correct statement of the law. In *Bernstein* itself it was held that the defendant did not trespass on Lord Bernstein's property by flying over it to take aerial photographs.

On the other hand, there has been held to be a trespass or nuisance where:

- a cornice overhung a neighbour's garden: *Fay v Prentice* (1845) 1 CB 828

- an advertising sign projected over a neighbour's property: *Gifford v Dent* [1926] WN 336 and *Kelsen v Imperial Tobacco Co (of Great Britain and Ireland) Ltd* [1957] 2 QB 334

- the booms of tower cranes oversailed the claimant's land: *Anchor Brewhouse Developments Ltd v Berkley House (Docklands Developments) Ltd* [1987] 2 EGLR 173

- an extractor fan projected over the claimant's yard: *Laiqat v Majid* [2005] EWHC 1305 (QB).

In a recent unreported case, *Anglo International Upholland Ltd v Wainwright and persons unknown* (2023, Unrep.) HHJ Bird sitting as a High Court Judge granted an interim injunction against the flying of drones by 'urban explorers' over the Claimant's derelict seminary building. However, in *MBR Acres v Free the MBR Beagles* [2021] EWHC 2996 (QB) Nicklin J refused to grant an interim injunction against the flying of drones over the Claimant's site (in order to take photographs) partly because it was uncertain whether that amounted to a trespass.

In addition to the limit on the vertical extent of ownership at common law described in *Bernstein of Leigh v Skyviews,* section 76(1) of the Civil Aviation Act 1982 provides that:

> "No action shall lie in respect of trespass or in respect of nuisance, by reason only of the flight of an aircraft over any property at a height above the ground which, having regard to wind, weather and all the circumstances of the case is reasonable, or the ordinary incidents of such flight, so long as the provisions of any Air Navigation Order and of any orders under section 62 above have been duly complied with".

The term 'aircraft' is not defined in the 1982 Act and there have been no judicial decisions as to whether section 76 applies to drones. However, drones are referred to as 'unmanned aircraft' in other legislation such as the Air Traffic Management and Unmanned Aircraft Act 2021. The Air Navigation Order 2016 (as amended) makes reference to unmanned aircraft in, for example, article 94A restricting flights of unmanned aircraft near aerodromes. Schedule 4, paragraph 1 of the Air Navigation Order 2016 defines a "remotely piloted aircraft" as an unmanned aircraft. So, it is likely that section 76 of the 1982 Act would be held to apply to drones, providing drone operators with immunity from trespass and nuisance actions so long as the drone is flown at a height which is reasonable in all the circumstances and in compliance with the Air Navigation Order 2016 etc.

S. 76 would not provide immunity from other possible causes of action, however, such as for harassment, misuse of private information or under the UK GDPR and Data Protection Act 2018 if, say, the drone is used to film individuals in their homes or gardens.

An unauthorised trespass into a neighbour's airspace will normally be restrained by injunction. See *Trenberth (John) Ltd v National Westminster Bank Ltd* (1979) 39 P & CR 104. However, the question whether the court will grant an injunction or damages in lieu of an injunction is a nuanced one. Historically, the courts have applied guidance given by A.L. Smith LJ in *Shelfer v City of London Electric Lighting Company* [1895] 1 Ch 287 where he put forward a 'good working rule' that damages can be granted in lieu of an injunction:

> "(1.) If the injury to the plaintiff's legal rights is small,

(2.) And is one which is capable of being estimated in money,

(3.) And is one which can be adequately compensated by a small money payment,

(4.) And the case is one in which it would be oppressive to the defendant to grant an injunction".

In *Coventry v Lawrence* [2014] UKSC 13, [2014] AC 822, the Supreme Court criticised what was described as an 'almost mechanical' application of that guidance in past cases and emphasised the breadth of the Court's discretion as to whether to award damages in lieu of injunction.

4. Statutory Regulation of Manned Flight Through Airspace

As indicated above, it has long been recognised that landowners' rights to the airspace above their land cannot be allowed to inhibit the use of that airspace, above a reasonable height, for powered flight. Aviation in the United Kingdom is regulated by the Civil Aviation Act 1982, the Airports Act 1986, the Transport Act 2000, the Civil Aviation Act 2012 and various statutory instruments including the Air Navigation Order 2016 and the Rules of the Air Regulations 2015. There is also much European Union law which affected United Kingdom air law and which became retained law following Brexit. This book is not the place for a detailed discussion of aviation law. Reference should be made to specialist texts for a full discussion of the statutory regimes affecting flight and the international agreements to which much of the legislation gives effect.

5. Dealings with freehold interests in airspace or subsoil

As will be discussed further in subsequent chapters, there is nothing to prevent the freehold owner of land carving out a horizontal division of it to sell, be that above or below the ground. The Law of Property Act 1925, s. 205(1)(ix) provides that "'Land" includes land of any tenure, and mines and minerals, whether or not held apart from the surface, buildings or parts of buildings (whether the division is horizontal, vertical or made in any other way) …'.

A freehold interest in an upper storey of a building is known as a "flying freehold". According to Lord Keith in *Sovmots Investments Ltd v Secretary of State for the Environment* [1979] AC 144 at 184:

> "Horizontally divided ownership of a building was extremely uncommon in England and Wales in 1957, being practically unknown… outside Lincoln's Inn. It is a conception which gives rise to a very complicated situation as regards the mutual rights and obligations of the several owners. It is, however, a conception familiar to the law of Scotland for centuries …".

Flying freeholds are not so uncommon now, although they are still comparatively rare.

Indeed, a flying freehold is capable of being acquired by adverse possession. See, for example, *Abbahall Ltd v Smee* [2003] 1 WLR 1472.

Even where the flying freehold is created by a conveyance or transfer there can be difficulties in regulating responsibility for maintenance and support. Positive covenants are not enforceable against subsequent owners; see *Rhone v Stephens*, [1994] 2 AC 310, a case concerning the roof of a house divided into flying freeholds. The principle of benefit and burden (a subsequent owner enjoying a benefit may be made subject to a reciprocal burden) will sometimes enable a positive covenant to be enforced by or against the owner of a flying freehold, but not always. The House of Lords decided that it did not assist the plaintiffs in *Rhone* who were seeking to enforce a covenant to repair the roof.

Absent any enforceable covenant, a common law duty in nuisance to take reasonable steps to prevent injury to a neighbour may require the owner of a flying freehold to contribute towards the cost of repair works; see *Abbahall Ltd v Smee* [2003] 1 WLR 1472.

Flying freeholds do not only exist above ground level, as the name suggests. There can also be a subterranean flying freehold where, for example, a cellar is conveyed or reserved separately to the house above it; see *Grigsby v Melville* [1974] 1 WLR 80 at 83. The existence of a subterranean flying freehold beneath a building may cause conveyancing difficulties for the building above if there are not clear rights of support in favour of the building and protection in respect of the subterranean layer.

Whether a particular parcel of land, or horizontal division of a parcel of land, is included in a conveyance is a mixed question of fact and law. In *Pennock v Hodgson* [2010] EWCA Civ 873 Mummery L.J. summarised the approach that the court takes to identifying boundaries as follows:

> "(1) The construction process starts with the conveyance which contains the parcels clause describing the relevant land, in this case the conveyance to the Defendant being first in time.
>
> (2) An attached plan stated to be "for the purposes of identification" does not define precise or exact boundaries. An attached plan based upon the Ordnance Survey, though usually very accurate, will not fix precise private boundaries nor will it always show every physical feature of the land.
>
> (3) Precise boundaries must be established by other evidence. That includes inferences from evidence of relevant physical features of the land existing and known at the time of the conveyance.
>
> (4) In principle there is no reason for preferring a line drawn on a plan based on the Ordnance Survey as evidence of the boundary to other relevant evidence that may lead the court to reject the plan as evidence of the boundary."

Normally, the plan to a conveyance will only show the outline of the land being sold at ground level, rendering it of little use if a question arises as to whether the parcel conveyed includes a subterranean level or a particular area above ground. The words of the parcels clause (the clause describing what is being conveyed) may make the position clear but, if not, the Court's starting position is likely to be as follows:

1. A conveyance of land ordinarily carries with it all that is beneath the surface (*Grigsby v Melville* [1974] 1 WLR 80 at 85 and 88, where a cellar was conveyed with the property above it even though the most convenient access was from a neighbouring property).

2. Since ownership of land normally carries with it the airspace above the land to such height as is necessary for the ordinary use and enjoyment of the land, a conveyance of land normally carries with it the whole of any building standing on it. In *Laybourn v Gridley* [1892] 2 Ch 53, for example, where part of a loft projected into the neighbouring property, it was held that the projecting part of the loft was conveyed as part of the neighbouring property.

3. Where the footings or eaves of a building extend beyond the boundary shown on a plan to a transfer separating the two parcels, the usual inference will be that they were intended to be included. Hence the transferee may acquire the footings and eaves but not the column of air between them. See *Truckell v Stock* [1957] 1 WLR 161.

A question that does not appear to have featured in many cases is whether a flying freehold comprising part of a building carries with it the airspace above or subsoil below the building. Consider a 3 storey building owned by A. A sells the freehold of the top floor including the roof to B, or of the ground floor to C, in either case retaining the other two floors. Does B acquire the airspace above the building or C the subsoil beneath it? Or do they remain with A who retains two-thirds of the building? Or are they somehow shared? The question would have to be approached by construing the conveyance to B or C. What, objectively speaking, were the intentions of the parties as to the vertical extent of the interest conveyed? Hence the question is essentially one of the boundary of the flying freehold sold, rendering it unlikely that A and B or C, as the case may be, would be held to share ownership of the subsoil or airspace unless the transfer expressly provides for joint ownership. If the terms of the transfer considered with the physical features of the land do not throw any light on the parties' intentions, the cuius est solum eius est usque ad coelum et ad inferos maxim may raise an inference that the subsoil was to go with freehold ownership of the bottom floor or airspace with freehold ownership of the top floor.

That is by no means the only possible inference, though. In *Corbett v Hill* (1869-70) LR 9 Eq 671 Sir William James V-C considered exactly this issue. C owned two adjoining houses and sold one of them to H. During redevelopment works by H it became apparent that a first-floor room retained by C projected into the house sold to H and was supported by it. Both parties claimed the air space above that room. The Vice-Chancellor held that H owned the air space. C retained the room (as a flying freehold) but owned nothing above or below it. The room was a diminution of H's ownership of the land and house that H had purchased, which otherwise extended upwards on the cuius est solum eius est usque ad coelum principle. Unfortunately, the judgment does not provide much explanation for why the Judge reached his conclusion. Nevertheless, in *Laybourn v Gridley* [1892] 2 Ch 53 (discussed in Chapter 3) North J said that he would have applied the decision in *Corbett* regarding the airspace above part of a loft alleged to comprise a flying freehold had he found the loft to be a flying freehold rather than within the ownership of the building beneath the loft.

In relation to subsoil, the fact that the whole building's foundations will be within the subsoil may point away from an inference that the subsoil goes with a flying freehold of the ground floor, as it has been held to do in the case of a lease of the ground floor (dealt with in the following chapter).

6. Highways

As Lord Briggs explained in *Southwark LBC v Transport for London* [2018] UKSC 63, [2020] AC 914, the word highway 'has no single meaning in the law but, in non-technical language, it is a way over which the public have rights of passage, whether on foot, on horseback or in (or on) vehicles'.

Highways may be adopted or unadopted. An adopted highway is one for which the relevant highway authority is responsible for maintenance. So, the majority of, but not all, made up roads will be adopted highways and some footpaths and bridleways will be adopted highways but many others will be unadopted.

The fact that a stretch of land qualifies as a highway does not affect ownership of airspace above or soil below the surface, but if the highway is an adopted one, then ownership of airspace and subsoil is affected.

A succession of nineteenth century highways acts – the Highways Act 1835, the Public Health Act 1848, the Metropolis Management Act 1855, the Public Health Act 1875 – all provided for a form of automatic vesting of a property interest in the land over which the adopted highway ran in favour of the body responsible for its maintenance and repair.

That property interest was restricted to that vertical slice of the plane containing the land over which the adopted highway runs which was necessary for its ordinary use and repair and maintenance; see *Tunbridge Wells Corpn v Baird* [1896] AC 434. The extent of that vertical slice includes the surface of the road over which the public had highway rights, the subsoil immediately beneath it to a depth sufficient to provide for its support and drainage (sometimes referred to as "the top two spits"), and a slice of the airspace above it sufficient to enable the public to use and enjoy the highway, and the responsible authority to maintain and repair it, and to supervise its safe operation. As Lord Briggs observed in the *Southwark LBC* case, the rule that the slice of property owned by the local authority is that required for ordinary use…

" … is a flexible concept, the application of which may lead to different depths of subsoil and heights of airspace being vested in a highway authority, both as between different highways and even, over time, as affects a particular highway, according to differences or changes in the nature and intensity of its public use. A simple footpath or bridleway might only require shallow foundations, and airspace of up to about ten feet, to accommodate someone riding a horse. By contrast a busy London street might require deep foundations to support intensive use, and airspace sufficient to accommodate double-decker buses, and even the overhead electric power cables needed, in the past, by trolley buses and, now, by urban trams."

Nowadays, that governing statutory provision is section 263 of the Highways Act 1980 which reads:

"(1) Subject to the provisions of this section, every highway maintainable at the public expense, together with the materials and scrapings of it, vests in the authority who are for the time being the highway authority for the highway.

"(2) Subsection (1) above does not apply— (a) to a highway with respect to the vesting of which, on its becoming or ceasing to be a trunk road, provision is made by section 265 below …"

S. 263 is subject to and reflects the principle described above that what vests in the highway authority is the vertical slice of land required for the highway's use and maintenance; see the *Southwark LBC* case at [12].

A consequence is that the subsoil beneath the highway will continue to vest in the owner of the land up to the level required by the highway authority for the support, drainage and maintenance of the surface. So, at common law the owner of the land containing the highway could tunnel under it and extract minerals provided that he does not remove support for the highway or interfere with apparatus laid under it by statutory undertakers (pipes, sewers, etc.); see e.g. *Cunliffe v Whalley*

(1851) 13 Beav 411.

Similarly, the owner of the land containing the highway owns the air above it and could erect, for example, wire above it so long as they do not interfere with the right of passage over the highway; see *Finchley Electric Light Co v Finchley UDC* [1903] 1 Ch 437.

That said, ss. 176 to 179 of the Highways Act 1980 prevent the owner of the subsoil from creating cellars and vaults under an adopted highway or erecting bridges, buildings, rails and beams over it without the consent of the highway authority.

It should also be noted that, while the usual position is as described above, highway authorities can acquire ownership of the whole land on which a highway sits, for example, by compulsory purchase for the purpose of building a road. In that case, of course, they will own the same amount of airspace and subsoil as any other owner of freehold land.

CHAPTER TWO

LEASEHOLD OWNERSHIP OF AIRSPACE AND SUBSOIL

1. Introduction

The question whether a lease of land containing a building includes the airspace above the building or the subsoil beneath it is one of interpretation of the lease. Broadly speaking, the Court takes the same approach to the construction of leases and other conveyances as is taken to contracts. That approach was helpfully summarised by Carr LJ in *Apache North Sea Ltd v Euroil Exploration Ltd* [2020] EWCA Civ 1397 at [33] to [34] as follows:

"33. Thus the court is concerned to identify the intention of the parties by reference to what a reasonable person having all the background knowledge which would have been available to the parties would have understood them to be using the language in the contract to mean. It does so by focusing on the meaning of the relevant words in their documentary, factual and commercial context. That meaning has to be assessed in the light of the natural and ordinary meaning of the clause, any other relevant provisions of the contract, the overall purpose of the clause and the contract, the facts and circumstances known or assumed by the parties at the time that the document was executed and commercial common sense, but disregarding the subjective evidence of the parties' intention. While commercial common sense is a very important factor to be taken into account, a court should be very slow to reject the natural meaning of a provision as correct simply because it appears to be a very imprudent term for one of the parties to have agreed. The meaning of a clause is usually most obviously to be gleaned from the language of the provision. Where the parties have used unambiguous language, the court must apply it; if there are two possible constructions, the court is entitled to prefer the construction consistent with common sense and to reject the other (see *Rainy Sky* (*supra*) at [21] and [23]).

34. In *Wood v Capita Insurance Services Ltd* (*supra*) at [9] to [11]) Lord Hodge JSC described the court's task as being to ascertain the objective meaning of the language which the parties have chosen to express their agreement. This is not a literalist exercise focused solely on a "parsing of the wording of the particular clause"; the court must consider the contract as a whole and, depending on the nature, formality and quality of drafting of the contract, give more or less weight to elements of the wider context in reaching its view as to that objective meaning. The interpretative exercise is a unitary one involving an iterative process by which each suggested interpretation is checked against the provisions of the contract and its commercial consequences investigated."

There are three glosses on that approach which are applied when the court is interpreting a conveyance or lease to ascertain exactly what property it conveys:

1. The Court will readily take into account the physical features on the ground at the date of the conveyance or lease, in the manner explained by Mummery LJ in *Pennock v Hodgson* [2010] EWCA Civ 873 in the passage quoted in section 1.5 above.

2. The court may take into account the subsequent conduct of the parties to the conveyance or lease (and possibly of successors-in-title) if that conduct is probative of the parties' intentions as to the extent of the parcel of land conveyed or leased, in a departure from the general rule that subsequent conduct is inadmissible on the question of how to construe a contract; see *Ali v Lane* [2006] EWCA Civ 1532.

3. As leases (if for over 7 years) and transfers of registered land are public documents obtainable from the Land Registry by prospective purchasers, when interpreting them little (if any) weight is to be given to background facts, such as the terms of

collateral documents, that would not be apparent from the transfer or lease itself and an inspection of the physical features of the land; see *Cherry Tree Investments v Landmain* [2012] EWCA Civ 736 at [124] to [130].

2. Airspace

If a lease demises airspace above a building, the tenant has the same right to restrain a trespass into that airspace as a freehold owner would have. For example, in *Kelsen v Imperial Tobacco Co. (of Great Britain and Ireland) Ltd* [1957] 2 QB 334 the lessee of a shop obtained an injunction to prevent a neighbouring property's advertising sign projecting into the airspace above the shop.

The more difficult question will often be whether the demise includes the airspace above the building. While the answer to that question will always turn on the construction of the particular lease, it is necessary to distinguish between three scenarios – a lease of a whole building, a lease of a vertical division of a building and a lease of a horizontal division of a building (i.e. of a flat or of one or more storeys of a multi-storey building).

Where the lease is of the whole building, including its roof, it will usually include the airspace above the land and building demised. In *Kelsen*, in which it was common ground that prima facie a lease of land includes the airspace above, McNair J commented that "prima facie, ... the lease of a single-storey ground floor premises would include the lease of the airspace above".

In *Straudley Investments Ltd v Barpress Ltd* [1987] 1 EGLR 69 there was a lease of "ALL THAT piece or parcel of ground with the messuages and buildings erected thereon situate and being on the South side of and Numbered 67, 69, 71, 73, 75, 77, 79 and 81 in Mortimer Street". The Court of Appeal considered it unarguable that the lease did not include the roof and airspace above of the buildings, so that the erection of a fire escape and erection duct across some of the roof was held to be a trespass.

In *Ravengate Estates Limited v Horizon Housing Group Limited* [2007] EWCA Civ 1368, which concerned the lease of the whole of a building except the ground and basement floors, Mann J, obiter, observed that there was a "presumption that a grant normally carries the airspace".

In *H Waites Ltd v Hambledon Court Ltd* [2014] EWHC 651 (Ch) Morgan J was concerned with a proposal to construct flats above a garage block comprising 12 garages, each let separately along with a corresponding flat. After the grant of the flat and garage leases, the freeholder had granted a lease of the airspace above the garages to the would-be developer. Morgan J held that the leases of the garages included the airspace above them. He surveyed a number of cases including those described above and concluded at [50]:

> "Whether one says that there is a presumption to be applied, I consider that where one is dealing with a demise of a building, where the wording of the demise is expressed by reference to a vertical division, and there is no wording expressing any horizontal division, it is natural to react to that wording by holding that there is no horizontal cut off which excludes the airspace above the building or, for that matter, the sub-soil below the building."

A recent example of the application of this approach is *Ralph Kline Ltd v Metropolitan and County Holdings Ltd* [2018] EWHC 64 (Ch), a decision of Edwin Johnson QC, sitting as a Deputy High Court Judge. The Defendant was lessee of a parade of shops with flats above and a garage below on the Finchley Road in north-west London, together with its gardens and grounds ("the Parade") under a 1970 lease ("the 1970 Lease"). Later, a reversionary lease of the Parade was granted by the freeholder which included the airspace above the buildings within the Parade. The lessee under the reversionary lease granted the Claimant a lease of the airspace above the buildings. The issue before the Court was whether the 1970 Lease to the Defendant included the airspace above the buildings, so that the airspace lease to the Claimant took effect subject to the 1970 Lease.

The judge first construed the 1970 Lease without reference to any of the authorities concerning airspace. His conclusion was that the demise included the entirety of the buildings within the Parade including their roofs. He stated a preliminary view that a letting of the whole of land and buildings, such as by the 1970 Lease, would normally include the airspace above them and that there was nothing in the 1970 Lease to lead to a different conclusion. Having reached his preliminary conclusion without reference to previous case law, the judge conducted a survey of authorities concerning the demise of the roof space. He observed that *Davies v Yadegar* (1990) 22 HLR 232 lends support to the proposition that if the lease includes the roofs it should also include the airspace above them, but was not prepare to derive from *Davies v Yadegar* a presumption that the demise of a roof is necessarily accompanied by a demise of the air space above it. However, drawing support from the *H Waites* decision, the judge concluded that the 1970 Lease carried with it the airspace above the Parade, so that the Claimant's airspace lease was merely reversionary.

Hence, where the lease is of an entire building or of a vertical division of a building that includes the roof (such as a terraced house or a garage within a garage block) unless the lease expressly shows a contrary intention the airspace above the building (or vertical division of the building) is likely to be included in the demise.

The outcome is less predictable where the lease is of a horizontal division of a building, i.e. a top floor flat or a top storey. The first question that will arise in such a case is whether the demise includes the roof. If not, it is unlikely to be held to include the airspace above the roof – such a discontinuous demise while theoretically possible is an improbable outcome.

Often the lease will not be explicit as to whether the demise includes the roof, leaving inferences to be drawn from such considerations as whether it is within the landlord's or tenant's repairing covenant, the physical layout and other factors that will vary from lease to lease and case to case. The outcome in such cases can be hard to predict. In *Delgable Ltd v Perinpanathan* [2005] EWCA Civ 1724, for example, a sub-lease of the top

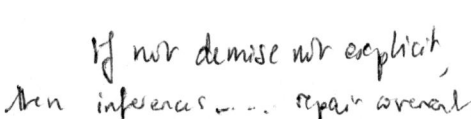

3 floors of a building was held to include the external walls but not the roof but Lloyd LJ commented that there was little to go on and so either result (the inclusion or exclusion of the roof in the demise) "might have been a reasonable one to aim for".

In *R (HCP (Hendon) Ltd) v Chief Land Registrar* [2020] 1 WLR 4240 a two-storey building was divided into 14 flats, seven on each floor. All the upper storey flat leases expressly stated that the roof was within the demise to the lessee but only three of those leases also stated that the roof space (between the roof of the building and the flat ceilings) was included. Martin Spencer J. rejected the 'somewhat bold submission' that he could conclude that the roof space had been included by mistake in the three flats which expressly included it because four did not. Notwithstanding that there was no express reference to the roof space in those four leases, the Judge interpreted them as including the roof space because it would make little sense to demise the roof but not the roof space.

Where the roof of the whole building is within the demise of the top floor lessee, it is likely to be held that the airspace above the roof is also within the premises demised to the top floor lessee, at least to a height that might be used for a loft extension of the like, unless the lease expressly provides otherwise. In *Davies v Yadegar* (1990) 22 HLR 232 a house was divided into an upper and a lower floor maisonette and the lease of the upper maisonette expressly included the loft space and roof. It was argued that the lessee of the upper maisonette was not entitled to carry out a loft conversion because she did not own the airspace above the roof and so would be trespassing by building a dormer window above the present roof line. The trial judge and the Court of Appeal found for the lessee. Woolf LJ said:

> "On a demise of this sort of premises which includes the roof space and the roof, the demise includes the air space above the roof and, accordingly, there is no trespass involved in carrying out an alteration which alters the profile of the roof so as to protrude further into the air space above the existing roof...

I can well see that, in a different situation where one is considering a block of flats containing a number of different premises occupied by different tenants where no tenant has included in his demise the roof, a position different from that which I have indicated could exist. However, in the situation that we are dealing with here of what was once a single residential unit which has been divided into two flats, in my view, Mr. Bickford-Smith's submission has no application. The roof space and the roof was included in the demise and the logical intent would be that the air space above should be included in that demise. Were the position otherwise one can easily see that all sorts of absurd results would follow: if the tenant of the upper flat wished to alter his chimney he would not be in a position to do so; if he wished to erect an aerial on the roof he would not be in a position to do so; if he wished to change the flow on the roof because of changes in building practices he would not be in a position to do so without the consent of the lessor, and the lessor would have a completely unfettered discretion to refuse that consent."

That said, there is probably no presumption as such in the case of horizontally divided buildings. In *Rosebery Ltd v Rocklee Ltd* [2011] L & TR 21, Nicholas Strauss QC sitting as a Deputy High Court Judge considered whether in the light of *Davies v Yadegar* there was a presumption that if a lease of part of a building includes the roof it also includes the airspace above the roof; he concluded that there was no presumption – that it is always a question of construction of the individual lease. As mentioned above, a similar conclusion was reached in the *Ralph Kline* case, although in the *Ralph Kline* case the judge endorsed Morgan J's conclusion that where the division is vertical rather than horizontal the airspace will usually be within the demise (see *H Waites Ltd v Hambledon Court Ltd* [2014] EWHC 651 (Ch)).

3. Subsoil

Just as with airspace, the question whether subsoil is included in a lease is a question of construction of the lease in question. While the increased popularity of residential basement excavations may yet generate a flurry of cases concerned with leasehold ownership of subsoil, there are at present only two such cases reported, in both of which it was held that the lessee did not own the subsoil.

In *Lejonvarn v Cromwell Mansions Management Company Ltd* [2011] EWHC 3838 (Ch) a house had been converted into three flats. The owners of the "ground floor, basement and cellar flat" wished to carry out works to extend the flat by excavating below ground, giving rise to the question whether the soil below the flat was included in the demise. John Jarvis QC, sitting as a Deputy High Court Judge, held that it was not. In reaching that conclusion he first of all analysed the lease and concluded that as a matter of construction it only demised the built-out areas known as the ground floor, basement and cellar flat. He then considered whether there was a presumption that the bottom floor flat carried with it the subsoil and concluded that it was not resolved by the authorities whether a presumption of ownership of subsoil applied to any particular lease. The judge considered that there was a distinction between subsoil and airspace because the subsoil will contain the whole building's foundations and so works by a lessee of part to the subsoil carry a risk to the rest of the building that works by a lessee of part to the roof would not carry. With that in mind, he held that the terms of the lease, which expressly placed repairing responsibility for the foundations, and the structure of the building, on the lessor led to the conclusion that the subsoil below the existing cellar and basement was not included in the demise of the ground floor, basement and cellar flat.

In *Gorst v Knight* [2018] EWHC 613 (Ch) HHJ Paul Matthews sitting as a Deputy High Court Judge reached a similar conclusion. He was concerned with the subsoil beneath a house in West London. The house was divided into two maisonettes. The Gorsts were lessees of the downstairs maisonette. Mrs Knight was the freeholder. The demise of the downstairs maisonette expressly included the foundations of the building and the cellar below the ground floor. That cellar was only half-height. The Gorsts wanted to dig it out by about another 4 feet in order to make it into a habitable room. The question in the case was whether that additional 4 feet of subsoil was within the demise of the downstairs maisonette, it being common ground that it was within the freehold title. If it was within the demise, Mrs Knight could not unreasonably refuse permission for the proposed works; if not, she could refuse permission as capriciously as she liked.

The Judge treated the issue as substantially a question of construction of the lease. He considered the presumption of ownership of airspace and subsoil discussed in chapter 1 and its application to leasehold land but concluded that in the case of a lease of a horizontal division of land there are no presumptions to be applied. Rather, the question is "what the construction of the grant, given what was available to be granted, and in the context, reveals the intentions of the parties [to the lease] to have been".

Counsel for the Gorsts sought to rely on *Davies v Yadegar*. HHJ Matthews held that there were important differences between airspace cases such as *Davies v Yadegar* and a subsoil case:

> "Chief among them is the fact that the subsoil is key to the stability of the whole building. If the foundations become unstable, the whole building is threatened. Not so of the roof. Second, access to the subsoil is more difficult, and will generally involve going through the lowest demise in the building. (I accept that *Bocardo* shows that this is not invariably so.) Thirdly, the subsoil is not visible and open to the elements, as the roof is. A problem with it will not be so easily noticed at an early stage. In my judgment, these considerations mean that one cannot apply authorities concerning the roof to the subsoil without further consideration."

On the particular facts of the case, it was held that the subsoil was not within the demise of the downstairs maisonette. The main pointers within the lease relied on by the Judge to reach his conclusion were:

1. That the demise referred to all parts of *the building* below the joists between the ground floor and first floor, whereas the subsoil was not part of *the building*

2. That the lease specifically extended the definition of the demise to include the cellar which otherwise might not fall within the definition of the building, the need for which extension suggested that the subsoil beneath the building would not otherwise be included

3. A reservation of a right to run services under the demised premises, suggesting that there is a lower limit to them, albeit that if the landlord retained possession of the subsoil she would not need a right to run services through it.

The Judge rejected a submission that the subsoil was included in the lease because the demise of the downstairs maisonette included "all parts of the building … below the line dividing equally the joists between the ground and first floors" on the grounds that the subsoil was not part of the building.

Martin Rodger QC, the Deputy Chamber President of the Upper Tribunal (Lands Chamber) endorsed that conclusion in *LM Homes v Queen Court Freehold Company Ltd* [2018] UKUT 367 (LC) in determining that the subsoil under a block of flats was not part of 'the building' for the purposes of a collective enfranchisement claim, albeit that it was within the 'common parts' for the purposes of the collective enfranchisement legislation contained in the part I of the Leasehold Reform, Housing and Urban Development Act 1993. When the *LM Homes* case was appealed to the Court of Appeal ([2020] EWCA Civ 371, [2020] QB 890), the Court held that the subsoil was part of 'the building' for the purposes of Part I of the 1993 Act but its reasons for that conclusion did not cast any doubt on the approach taken in *Gorst* to the question whether subsoil is demised.

See chapter 5 below for a fuller discussion of the *LM Homes* case.

4. Summary

The following tentative conclusions can be drawn from the cases discussed above:

1. Whether a lease of a building or part of a building includes the airspace above or subsoil below the building is a question of interpretation of the lease in question, in particular the parcels clause which sets out what is included in the lease; 'interpretation' in this context means the ascertainment of the *objective* meaning of the language which the parties have chosen in which to express their agreement.

2. There are probably no presumptions as such to be applied but certain conclusions are more likely than others (if the lease does not make express provision about ownership of airspace or subsoil as leases tend not to do).

3. If the lease is of the whole building, it will probably include the airspace above and subsoil beneath unless there is some particular reason for the court to conclude that the parties to the lease intended otherwise.

4. If the lease is of a vertical division of the building, it is fairly likely to include the airspace above and subsoil beneath unless there is some particular reason for the court to conclude that the parties to the lease intended otherwise.

5. If the lease is of a horizontal division of a building – a flat or a storey or part of a storey – the outcome is less predictable and will depend on the particular lease and the particular building.

6. The inclusion of the roof and roof space within a demise of the

whole of a top floor will often carry with it the airspace, unless there is some specific reason to conclude that it does not.

7. A lease of only part of the top floor is less likely to include airspace than a lease of the whole top floor.

8. If the roof is retained by the lessor, the lease probably does not demise the airspace above the roof.

9. The inclusion of the foundations and/or a basement within the demise of the ground floor in a lease of ground floor premises is not entirely comparable to the inclusion of the roof in the demise of a top floor because of the effect that works to the subsoil might have to the stability of the building. It does not necessarily suggest that the subsoil was intended to be included in the demise.

10. The risk of destabilising the whole building by works to the subsoil may make the courts more reluctant to conclude that subsoil goes with a ground floor demise than they are to conclude that airspace goes with a top floor demise.

That having been said, points (3) to (10) above can only be generalisations. There is no substitute for analysis of the terms of the particular lease and consideration of the layout of the building and other relevant background facts in order to ascertain the meaning of the parcels clause in the lease.

The lease of a house, or a headlease of an entire block of flats, is more likely to include the subsoil than a lease of a ground or basement floor flat.

CHAPTER THREE

CONVEYANCING AND LAND REGISTRATION

1. Land Registration

More than ordinary care should be taken when preparing a conveyance of airspace or subsoil separately from the building below or above it. Not only is it important to include all appropriate rights such as of shelter and support but it is crucial that the transfer or lease contains a precise description or depiction of the area to be conveyed.

Rule 24(1) of the Land Registration Rules 2003 contains the general requirement that any application for first registration should include "sufficient details, by plan or otherwise (subject to rules 25 and 26), so that the land can be identified clearly on the Ordnance Survey map".

Rule 26(1) of the Land Registration Rules 2003 is headed "First registration of cellars, flats, tunnels etc" and reads as follows:

> "(1) Subject to paragraph (2) [which concerns exclusion of mines and minerals from an application for registration], unless all of the land above and below the surface is included in an application for first registration the applicant must provide a plan of the surface on under or over which the land to be registered lies, and sufficient information to define the vertical and horizontal extents of the land."

The Land Registry's published guidance for preparing plans for Land Registry applications (Practice Guide 40, Supplement 2) deals with application for first registration of airspace or sub-soil at paragraph 6. It makes the point that the Land Registry has to be given a clear understanding of what is to be registered and that invariably a plan is required. With respect to airspace or subsoil the Land Registry needs to be told where the area being conveyed lies in relation to the features on the ground as well as the depth or height of the land being conveyed (or excluded from a conveyance). As the Land Registry guidance helpfully points out, Ordnance Survey datum can be used to define height to fine tolerances.

Of course, if the land (or airspace or subsoil) in question is already registered, and the whole title is being sold, there is no need to spell out exactly what is being conveyed again. It can safely be conveyed by reference to the registered title number. On the other hand, when only part of a registered title is being transferred, by Form TP1, the same need to precisely define any strata of airspace or subsoil being transferred separately arises as it does on first registrations.

Where a registered title includes only a horizontal section of land, say a first floor flat, the register will contain a note to the effect that only the first floor flat (or as the case may be) is included in the title. In *R (HCP (Hendon) Ltd) v Chief Land Registrar* [2020] 1 WLR 4240 it was argued that a note of that sort can be relied on as establishing the vertical limit of the title, so that if the lease would include the roof of the building or airspace above a first floor flat as a matter of interpretation, but the register notes that only the first floor flat is included in the title, the roof and airspace is not included in the registered title. Perhaps unsurprisingly, that submission was rejected by Martin Spencer J. who held:

> "30. … where a purchaser or someone otherwise inspecting the register of freehold property which includes in the charges register reference to registered leases and wishes to ascertain whether the roof or roof space is included in the registered title, that person needs to inspect the leases and cannot rely simply on what is contained on the face of the register."

When seeking to draw conclusions about the extent of land included within a registered title it is also necessary to bear in mind the general boundaries rule contained in section 60 of the Land Registration Act 2002. That is to the effect that unless the exact line of a boundary has been determined, the register only shows general boundaries, and a general boundary does not show the exact line of the boundary. The vast majority of boundaries shown on registered title plans are general boundaries, not determined boundaries.

2. Conveyancing in Relation to Airspace or Subsoil Generally

Those solicitors, barristers and surveyors whose practice encompasses boundary disputes will be familiar with the many ways in which a transfer or lease can leave room for future dispute about the precise extent of the land conveyed or let: poor quality and out-of-date plans; lines to delineate the area conveyed drawn so thickly on small-scale plans as to cover metres on the ground; measurements that are inconsistent with the delineating lines on the plan; verbal descriptions that convey no useful information or, worse still, contradict the plan. In *Scarfe v Adams* [1981] 1 All ER 843, CA Cumming-Bruce LJ discussed what he described as a cautionary tale arising from an inadequate transfer of part. He observed

> "I hope that this judgment will be understood by every conveyancing solicitor in the land as giving them warning, loud and clear, that a conveyancing technique which may have been effective in the old days to convey large property from one vendor to one purchaser will lead to nothing but trouble, disputes, and expensive litigation if applied to the sale to separate purchasers of a single house and its curtilage divided into separate parts. For such purposes it is absolutely essential that each parcel conveyed shall be described in the conveyance or transfer deed with such particularity and precision that there is no room for doubt about the boundaries of each, and for such purposes if a plan is intended to control the description, an Ordnance map on a scale of 1:2500 is worse than useless. The plan or other drawing bound up with the deed must be on such a large scale that it clearly shows with precision where each boundary runs. In my view the parties to this appeal are the victims of sloppy conveyancing for

which the professional advisers of vendor and purchasers appear to bear the responsibility. We are not concerned in this appeal with determining or apportioning that responsibility. This court has to try to reduce to order the confusion created by the conveyancers."

In *Truckell v Stock* [1957] 1 WLR 161, the question arose whether the footings of the plaintiff's house had been conveyed to him even though the conveyance plan showed the boundary of the land conveyed as the outer face of the wall and the footings projected beyond that face. Ownership of the footings mattered because the defendant had built a wall resting on them and the plaintiff had sued in trespass. At first instance the plaintiff's claim failed on the basis that the footings, being outside the area shown as conveyed by the relevant plan, did not belong to the plaintiff and so the defendant could not be trespassing on them. In the Court of Appeal the plaintiff succeeded on the grounds that what was conveyed to the plaintiff was his building including its footings. So, the plaintiff's property "included not only the walls but the eaves and the footings of the house. It did not include the column of air between the footings and the eaves, but it included the footings and the eaves". Hodson LJ commented:

> "the plan is a ground plan and only shows the boundary of the plaintiff's property on the ground; whereas the conveyance of the house and the parcels show the actual physical thing conveyed. That a property — a house — may stick out over the land of the adjoining neighbour is a common feature which has caused trouble, as shown by the reported cases"

It goes without saying, that a precise verbal and/or graphical description of what is being conveyed in a conveyance or lease is the best means of avoiding that trouble, especially where horizontal strata or airspace or subsoil are not being conveyed with all the strata above or below them.

An example of a case where that did not occur is *Turner v Wakefield* [2004] EWCA Civ 1725 in which a mother conveyed part of her land to her son and part to her daughter by two separate transfers. The mother's land included a barn and the two transfers showed an intention to convey part of the barn to the son and part to the daughter, but did not adequately make clear the dividing line. The Court of Appeal held that in the light of the prior usage and internal configuration of the barn, the dividing line at first floor level was different to that at ground floor level, creating a flying freehold of part of the first floor.

In contrast to *Turner* is *Laybourn v Gridley* [1892] 2 Ch 53. In the latter case, there were two adjacent wooden buildings and the loft over one of them extended for a small part over the other. Both buildings were sold, the land comprising the second building being sold first by a conveyance to the plaintiffs' predecessors with a plan attached showing a boundary line which if projected to first floor level would appear to include in the conveyance that part of the loft situated over the second building. The other building was then sold to the defendants' predecessor with a conveyance plan which showed the boundary of the land sold at ground floor level only, i.e. not showing the first floor projection of the loft into the adjoining building included in the conveyance. In fact, the whole of the loft was occupied with the defendants' building at the time of the conveyances. The defendants contended that the part over the other building had been acquired by their predecessor in the light of its occupation with their building. North J rejected that contention, dividing the loft along the line of the ground floor separation between the buildings.

It should be borne in mind that the UK Finance Mortgage Lenders' Handbook for conveyancers (the CML Handbook as it used to be known) has specific requirements for flying freeholds in section 5.7. Not all lenders represented by UK Finance will lend on flying freeholds and those that do may have specific requirements regarding them. There are also specific provisions in section 5.20 dealing with leases of roof space for solar PV panels.

3. Conveyancing of Interests in Mines and Minerals

So far as mines and minerals beneath the surface go, they are treated as included in a sale unless the contract stipulates otherwise, with the exception of gold, silver, petroleum and coal. See *Bellamy v Debenham* [1891] 1 Ch 412.

Rule 25 of the Land Registration Rules 2003 deals with first registration of an interest in mines and minerals and reads:

> "25. First registration of mines and minerals
>
> When applying for first registration of an estate in mines and minerals held apart from the surface, the applicant must provide–
>
> (a) a plan of the surface under which the mines and minerals lie,
>
> (b) any other sufficient details by plan or otherwise so that the mines and minerals can be identified clearly, and
>
> (c) full details of rights incidental to the working of the mines and minerals."

On first registration of an estate, the Registrar is obliged to make a note in the register if satisfied that the mines and minerals are included in the title (Land Registration Rules 2003, r. 32). A similar note can be made later if the Registrar is satisfied at a later date of the inclusion of the mines and minerals. Absent such a note, no indemnity under Sch. 8 of the Land Registration Act 2002 is payable in respect of mines and minerals where a right to indemnity arises out of a mistake in the register (para. 2 of Sch. 8).

At present, registration of an estate in mines and minerals is not compulsory but the Law Commission has proposed amending the Act to make it compulsory.

4. Liens Over Airspace

It is a feature of modern-day homebuying that purchasers sometimes agree to buy flats off-plan in blocks of flats that have yet to be built. Of course, a deposit will have been paid on exchange of contract. What happens if the developer becomes insolvent and the block of flats is not built? What interest do the purchasers have in the airspace which their flat was to occupy? In particular, do the purchasers acquire an equitable lien over that airspace?

The answer to this question is not an academic one. It will make the difference between the purchasers having the status of secured as opposed to unsecured creditor in the insolvency of the developer which may make a real difference to their prospects of recovering their deposits. As Arnold J put it in *Eason v Wong* [2017] EWHC 209 (Ch) at [15]:

> "An equitable lien is an equitable right over real or personal property to secure the discharge of a debt. An equitable lien is a form of equitable charge over the subject property. Both an equitable lien and an equitable charge are enforceable by the same remedies, namely by the appointment by the court of a receiver and a judicial order for sale or, where the security is over a fund, by an order for payment from the fund. An equitable lien, like an equitable charge, confers on the holder a proprietary right, so that he is a secured creditor in a bankruptcy or winding up."

In *Eason* the developer of a block of flats had become insolvent before construction began on the block of flats in which the claimants had contracted to buy flats. The site was sold by the developer's liquidators and the question before the Court was whether purchasers of flats in the unbuilt block were to be treated as secured creditors of the developer by reason of having equitable liens. The developer's liquidators denied that the purchasers had enforceable equitable liens on the ground that the liens would be over leases never created of parts of a building that had not been built. Arnold J rejected the liquidators' argument. He held that "the subject matter of each contract was in effect the legal estate in the relevant air space which would have been occupied by the Suite when constructed" and that this was not an obstacle to the purchasers acquiring equitable liens over the developers' freehold interest in the airspace which was the subject of each contract. Hence the purchasers were entitled as secured creditors to share pro rata in the proceeds of sale of the site.

Williams, Armstrong v Alter Domus Trustees (UK) Ltd [2023] EWHC 1820 (Ch) concerned a failed mixed-use development that would have included adding new storeys about the existing building. Purchasers off-plan of flats within the floors that were not built contended that they held equitable liens over the entire site but Miles J., following *Eason*, held that each purchaser's lien attached to the airspace that would have been occupied by the flat that they had contracted to buy.

CHAPTER FOUR

EASEMENTS AFFECTING AIRSPACE AND SUBSOIL

1. Introduction

Easements are, as the reader is likely to know, rights over one parcel of land for the benefit of another parcel of land. An easement may be a right to do something such as a right of way, or a right to prevent something such as a right to light (which is best seen as a right to prevent obstruction of light).

An easement may be acquired:

1. by express grant or reservation,

2. by implied grant or (less commonly) implied reservation,

3. by the operation of general words under s. 62 of the Law of Property Act 1925,

4. by prescription, i.e. long use, or

5. by statute.

For a right to qualify as an easement it must be of a nature that could form the subject-matter of an express grant, even if it is acquired by implication, general words or prescription.

In broad terms, to qualify as an easement a right must:

1. benefit a parcel of land (the dominant land) which is close enough to the land subject to the right (the servient land) for the dominant land to obtain a practical benefit from the right

2. be created when the dominant land and servient land are not owned and occupied by the same person

3. be within the general nature of rights capable of being created as easements

4. not require the owner of the servient land to expend money (with some exceptions such as fencing easements)

5. not be so extensive as to deprive the owner of the servient land of all reasonable use of it or to amount to possession of the servient land

6. be capable of reasonably exact definition.

The most commonly encountered easement is probably the right of way but for the purposes of this book there are four categories of easement that are especially important, two affecting subsoil and two affecting airspace. They are (1) support, (2) drainage and rights in respect of underground water, (3) air and (4) light. They will be discussed in turn below.

2. Acquisition of Easements

For a full discussion of the means by which easements are acquired, the reader should consult a specialist text such as Gale on the Law of Easements (Sweet & Maxwell). Only an introductory outline is provided in the following paragraphs.

In summary, easements can be expressly granted to a transferee or lessee or reserved by a transferor or lessor, in a transfer of land or a lease. Or they can be granted in a separate deed of easement. If expressly granted or reserved, other than in a will, they must usually be contained in a deed to take effect as legal easements (see s. 52 of the Law of Property Act 1925). And if the servient land is registered the grant or reservation must be completed by registration under the Land Registration Act 2002 in order to take effect as a legal, rather than equitable, easement[2].

Even where a conveyance does not create an easement by express words, it may do so by the operation of s. 62 of the Law of Property Act 1925. That section provides that, if there is no contrary intention expressed, every conveyance of land includes "all…liberties, privileges, easements, rights, and advantages whatsoever, appertaining or reputed to appertain to the land, or any part thereof, or, at the time of conveyance,…enjoyed with…the land or any part thereof". S. 62 operates to convert into easements rights capable of being easements that were enjoyed by licence or that were exercised without any clear origin at the time of the conveyance. For it to operate the dominant and servient land must have been in separate occupation (e.g. where the servient land is occupied by a lessee) or the right must be a continuous and apparent "quasi-easement" such as to light or to use a watercourse.

Easements can also be granted (but not usually reserved) by implication. An easement might arise by implication out of necessity (e.g. where land is sold which would by landlocked if a right of way of necessity were not implied). An easement might be granted by implication to give effect to a common intention that the property being acquired should be used in a particular way for which the easement is necessary; for a recent example see *Linvale Investment Ltd v Walker* [2016] 2 P & CR 12.

Easements may arise by implication under the rule in *Wheeldon v Burrows* (1879) 12 Ch D 31. That rule applies to "quasi-easements" which were in use before land was divided into separate ownership, and converts the quasi-easement into an easement when part of the land is sold off. For the rule to apply the quasi-easement must be (i) continuous and apparent, (ii) necessary for the reasonable enjoyment of the land sold and (iii) used by the vendor for the benefit of the land sold before and at the time of the sale.

---

[2] The main practical difference between a legal easement and an equitable easement is that the former will almost always bind third-party purchasers but the latter may not.

Often, it will be easier to meet the requirements of s. 62 than those of the rule in *Wheeldon v Burrows*.

In order to obtain an easement by prescription, at common law or under the doctrine of lost modern grant or under the Prescription Act 1832 it is necessary for the claimant or the claimant and their predecessor(s)-in-title to have enjoyed the right for a continuous period of at least 20 years 'as of right', that is uncontentiously, openly and without permission (nec vi nec clam nec precario in the old Latin phrase).

To acquire an easement by prescription at common law use since time immemorial (arbitrarily designated as since 1189) must be shown. Although proof of use for 20 years is presumed to have originated since time immemorial, that presumption can be rebutted by proving that at some time after 1189 the right did not or could not exist. For example, it might be proved that a building could not have acquired a right to light at common law because it had been built after 1189.

Because of the difficulties associated with proving sufficiently long user at common law, the courts developed the doctrine of lost modern grant under which it is assumed that there must have been some express grant of the right which has been lost if user for 20 years is proved. The presumption of lost modern grant is not rebutted by proof that in fact there was not such a grant. See *Dalton v Angus & Co* (1881) 6 App Cas 740 and *Tehidy Minerals Ltd v Norman* [1971] 2 QB 528.

Where its requirements are met, the Prescription Act 1832 provides an alternative to common law prescription and the doctrine of lost modern grant. Under the 1832 Act there must be proof of the prescribed period of user as of right continuing until the issue of proceedings ("next before suit or action"). However, the act provides that no act is deemed to be an interruption of the period of use until it has been submitted to or acquiesced in for a year. The Act requires a period of 20 years' use but also provides that if 40 years' use is shown, the easement is deemed absolute and indefeasible unless enjoyed by written consent. So oral permission will not defeat a claim under the Act based on 40 years' user or more if the oral permission was given at the beginning of the period of user (although oral permission given during the 40 year period would do so); see *Gardner v Hodgson's Kingston Brewery Co Ltd* [1901] 2 Ch. 198; [1903] A.C. 229.

The 1832 Act also treats easements of lights differently. In respect of easements of light, 20 years user will establish the easement unless it is with written consent, and even if it is not user 'as of right', e.g. because of oral permission given during the period of use.

For a comprehensive treatment of the 1832 Act and of easements generally, readers are referred to specialist works such as the one mentioned above.

3. Easements of Support

The natural right to support of land by other land

Ownership of land carries with it a natural right of support for the soil from adjacent land. There is the same right of support from the strata of land below if in different ownership (as in *Humphries v Brogden* (1850) 12 QB 739 where the plaintiff's land at the surface was damaged by the defendant's mining operations beneath it).

The right for support of soil, as opposed to buildings, is a right of property incidental to ownership of land and it is not necessary to prove its acquisition as an easement; see *Bonomi v Backhouse* (1858) El Bl & El 622. That right does not apply to buildings per se, but if a building is damaged by a withdrawal of support that would have affected the land it stood on anyhow, damages can be recovered for the loss to the building; see *Stroyan v Knowles* (1861) 6 Hurl & N 454. On the other hand, if the land would not have been materially affected by the withdrawal of support had the building not been there, the natural right for support of the soil cannot be relied on to justify a claim for damage to the building; see, for example, *Ray v Fairway Motors (Barnstaple) Ltd* (1969) 20 P & CR 261.

As a matter of property law the right is a negative one, not to have support removed. However, in some circumstances there may also be a positive, measured duty of care in tort to take action to prevent foreseeable damage to a neighbouring owner as a result of naturally occurring loss of support. See *Holbeck Hall Hotel Ltd v Scarborough Borough Council* [2000] QB 836 which concerned damage to the claimant's cliff-top hotel arising from a landslip on the undercliff owned by the defendant; it was held that the defendant did owe the claimant a limited duty of care but that the defendant was not in breach of it.

This natural right of support prevents the adjacent or subjacent neighbour from causing damage by removing soil from their own land. It does not prevent damage being caused by extraction of water. There is no common law right of support from any water there might be in the neighbouring soil and no common law impediment to draining land even though that might damage neighbouring land; see *Popplewell v Hodkinson* (1868-69) LR 4 Ex 248.

This rule relates to water narrowly defined, though. It has been held not to apply to silt or other substances mixed with water such as saturated brine. Hence, in *Lotus Ltd v British Soda Co. Ltd* [1972] Ch 123 the defendant salt producer was held liable for damage to the claimant's factory resulting from subsidence arising when the defendant pumped brine from its own land causing salt under the claimant's land to be dissolved in the water that was drawn under that land by the defendant's pumping operation.

While there is no common law right to support by water, there is a statutory obligation not to cause damage to another person by abstracting water from inland waters or underground strata contained in section 48A of the Water Resources Act 1991. Liability under that provision is strict – negligence need not be proved – albeit it is subject to exceptions for some activities licenced under the Act [section 48A(7)].

Acquired rights of support for buildings

While buildings do not have a natural right of support, an easement of support for a building from adjacent or subjacent land can be acquired by prescription as a result of 20 years' enjoyment of support as of right; see *Dalton v Angus* (1881) 6 App Ca 740. Thus, once it is shown that a building has been supported by neighbouring land for 20 years, openly, not contentiously or by permission, the building acquires the right to continue to be supported. And of course a right of support can be expressly or impliedly granted too, and can be acquired under s. 62 of the Law of Property Act 1925.

Not only can a building acquire a right of support from neighbouring land, it can also acquire a right of support from a neighbouring building. Such a right may arise by prescription as in *Lemaitre v Davis* (1881) 19 Ch D 281 or by express or implied grant or under s. 62 of the Law of Property Act 1925.

The right of support for buildings acquired by prescription or implication is essentially the same as the natural right to support for land; that is, it is a right not to have the support previously enjoyed actively removed. In *Bond v Nottingham Corporation* [1940] Ch 429, Sir Wilfred Greene MR said:

> "The nature of the right of support is not open to dispute. The owner of the servient tenement is under no obligation to repair that part of his building which provides support for his neighbour. He can let it fall into decay. If it does so, and support is removed, the owner of the dominant tenement has no cause for complaint. On the other hand, the owner of the dominant tenement is not bound to sit by and watch the gradual deterioration of the support constituted by his neighbour's building. He is entitled to enter and take the necessary steps to ensure that the support continues by effecting repairs, and so forth, to the part of the building which gives the support. But what the owner of the servient tenement is

not entitled to do is, by an act of his own, to remove the support without providing an equivalent."

The extent and effect of a right of support granted by express words will be a question of interpretation of the conveyance, lease or deed granting it.

4. Pipes, Drains and Underground Water

The stratum below the surface will not always contain subsoil alone, of course. Putting aside minerals and the like, the subject of another chapter, it may contain pipes, cables, drains and other conduits. There may be underground water running through it in a defined channel or through undefined, or at least unknown, channels.

<u>Pipes, drains and other conduits</u>

Easements to lay or use a pipe or other conduit, or to a supply of water (or gas, or electricity) or to discharge foul water and the right to enter on servient land to repair or replace a pipe or other conduit are all capable of being expressly granted or reserved, impliedly granted or (more rarely) reserved, obtained under s. 62 of the Law of Property Act 1925 or established by prescription.

Where the right in question is expressly granted or reserved, it will be a question of interpretation of the grant or reservation whether, for example, the right is to a supply of water or merely the passage through the pipe of such water as there might be, or whether the right to maintain a pipe under the servient land includes a right to replace it with a larger pipe.

For example, in *Rance v Elvin* (1985) 50 P & CR 9, R purchased his property with the benefit of a right "to the free and uninterrupted passage and running of water soil gas and electricity through the sewers drains and watercourses and water gas and electric pipes wires and cables … in or under ... the vendor's adjoining or neighbouring land or premises (the purchaser bearing paying and contributing together with the vendor or the other owner or owners aforesaid a fair proportion according to the extent which the same are served thereby of the cost of repairing maintaining renewing and cleansing the water gas and electricity services)". Water was supplied via a water meter on the retained land and the owner of the retained land had to pay the water company for it. A dispute arose as to whether there was a right of water supply in favour of R which obliged the servient owner to pay the water company. Easements do not usually impose positive obligations on the servient owner. The Court of Appeal held that R's easement was limited to the passage of any water coming into the pipes on the retained land through those pipes to R's land. Any physical interference with the passage of such water would be an actionable interference with the easement. But the owner of the retained land was under no obligation to ensure that any water comes into those pipes. There was no right to a supply. So, there was no obligation to pay the water company although R could make his own arrangements to pay if the servient owner ceased doing so.

A dominant owner with the right to use a pipe (or other conduit) will have an incidental right to come on to the servient land to repair or maintain it, but the servient owner will not be under any such obligation (unless expressly imposed). See *Duke of Westminster v Guild* [1985] 1 QB 688. Whether the dominant owner can not only repair the pipe but replace it with a larger one or divert it will depend on the terms of the grant or reservation of the right. For an example, consider *Coopind (UK) Ltd v Walton Commercial Group Ltd* [1989] 1 EGLR 241.

Where there is no express grant there may be an implied or prescriptive easement. Where the owner of two adjoining houses sells one of them, there will be an implied grant of an easement to use any drains serving the house sold passing through the land retained, even though the drains may not be "apparent" in the sense of being visible. It is enough if it must have been obvious that some drainage existed. See *Pyer v Carter* (1857) 1 Hurl & N 916. More recently, in *Donovan v Rana* [2014] EWCA Civ 99, [2014] 1 P & CR 23 there was implied into a transfer of a building plot in a suburban area a right to lay drainage, water, gas, electricity and telephone connections through land retained by the vendor to reach the main services under the highway. The Court of Appeal upheld the trial judge's finding that an easement to that effect could be implied from the common intention of the parties that the building plot was being sold in order that a house could be erected on it.

In relation to a claim to a prescriptive right to use of a drain that has been in use for 20 years or more, the crucial question is likely to be whether the use was or ought to have been known about by the servient owner. In *Barney v BP Truckstops* [1995] NPC 5 a claim to a prescriptive right of sewerage was defeated because the use of the pipe through the servient land, while not surreptitious, was unknown to the servient owner.

In addition to private rights by way of easements, subsoil may be subject to statutory rights in relation to installations for the supply and discharge of water (under the Water Resources Act 1991 and the Water Industry Act 1991) and gas (under the Gas Act 1986). There may be wayleaves for electricity cables above and below ground under the Electricity Act 1989. The Electronic Communications Code which took effect in December 2017 provides electronic communications network operators with extensive rights to install and maintain electronic communications apparatus on, under or over private land.

Underground water

If there is a natural underground stream flowing under A's land through a defined, known channel, A as freeholder will have certain natural, common law rights to it, just as A would if the stream was on the surface. Those rights are the right to use the water for certain purposes, the right to have the water flow into his land without obstruction and the right for the water not to be polluted. A corollary of those rights is an obligation to those downstream to A not to obstruct or pollute the stream.

If there is underground water under A's land which is not flowing through a known defined channel the same rules do not apply. At common law, water in undefined and unknown channels can be diverted or appropriated without there being any liability to owners downstream, see *Rugby Joint Water Board v Walters* [1967] Ch 397. However, the common law position has been altered by section 48A of the Water Resources Act 1991 discussed in section 3 of this chapter above.

5. Rights of Air

It is long-established that there is no easement of prospect or view; see *Hunter v Canary Wharf Ltd* [1997] AC 655, 709. That said, while there is no right to an attractive view, the sight of something offensive on neighbouring land is in principle capable of being an actionable nuisance; see *Fearn v Board of Trustees of Tate Gallery* [2023] UKSC 4, [2023] 2 WLR 339 at [15]. Furthermore, as the *Fearn* case established (to the surprise of many), the law of nuisance can be relied on to prevent visual intrusion from one property to another. In that case it was held that owners of glass-walled flats overlooked from the viewing gallery of the Tate Modern art gallery in London were caused an actionable nuisance by the many visitors to the viewing gallery peering into their homes. It was important in that case that a viewing gallery was held not to be an ordinary use of the Tate Modern's land. Overlooking in the course of ordinary use of land would not amount to a nuisance.

There is no right to the access of air passing over the general surface of neighbouring land, for example the uninterrupted flow of undefined air to a chimney (as in *Bryant v Lefever* (1879) 4 CPD 172) or a windmill (as in *Webb v Bird* (1861) 10 CB (ns) 268). A landowner wanting to protect the flow of air to their land will have to take out a restrictive covenant preventing a neighbouring owner from building so as to interfere with the flow of air.

On the other hand, it is possible to acquire by prescription a right to the flow of air to a definite aperture, e.g. a window, or through a definite channel over neighbouring land. For example, in *Bass v Gregory* (1890) 25 QBD 481 it was held that the owners of a public house had acquired by prescription a right to the passage of air into their cellar via a shaft leading to a disused well in a neighbouring yard.

Occasionally, it may be possible to pray in aid the principle of non-derogation from grant in support of a claim to the right of air. That principle, in essence one of fair-dealing, restrains a grantor of land from doing something on land retained by the grantor which substantially interferes with the enjoyment of the land granted. It was successfully relied on in *Cable v Bryant* [1908] 1 Ch 259 to prevent a vendor of land with stables on it from erecting a hoarding on retained land which obscured apertures through which the stables were ventilated.

A recent and unusual example of an expressly granted right affecting air is the decision in *Bockenfield Aerodrome Ltd v Clarehugh* [2021] EWHC 848 (Ch), [2022] 1 P & CR 17. A 1993 conveyance of an airfield contained a grant of "the unrestricted right to use at a safe height the airspace above the retained land for the passage of aircraft in circuit arriving or leaving the property". At the time the retained land was made up of open fields. It was later acquired by the defendants who ran a woodland burials service from it and maintained 12,000 trees on the land that was subject to the right to use for the passage of aircraft. The height of the trees made take-off and landing from the airstrip more difficult and disrupted airflow so as to impact aircraft stability. The court ordered that the trees be cut back or removed so as to allow safer aircraft manoeuvring.

6. Rights of Light

There is no automatic right to light, i.e. to have one's windows not darkened by a neighbouring building. However, a right to light can be acquired as an easement by express or implied grant, or by prescription after 20 years of unobstructed use of a window or other similar aperture. A right to light acquired by prescription is sometimes referred to as "ancient lights". Like other prescriptive easements, a right to light can be acquired at common law (unusually), by lost modern grant or under the Prescription Act 1832 (s. 3 of the 1832 Act deals with rights to light).

A right to light is a right in favour of a building, not a vacant lot, and in particular the apertures in the building for letting in light. So, it applies not only to windows but also to skylights. It does not apply to an ordinary door (see *Levet v Gas Light and Coke Co.* [1919] 1 Ch 24) but would, presumably, apply to glass doors designed to let in light as well as functioning as doors. It has been held to apply to the panels in greenhouse; see *Allen v Greenwood* [1980] Ch 119.

Whether there is an actionable interference with a right to light is determined by considering how much light the dominant owner has left, not how much has been lost as a result of the erection of the structure to which objection is taken. It was established by the House of Lords in *Colls v Home and Colonial Stores Ltd* [1904] AC1 79 that:

> "generally speaking an owner of ancient lights is entitled to sufficient light according to the ordinary notions of mankind for the comfortable use and enjoyment of his house as a dwelling-house, if it is a dwelling-house, or for the beneficial use and occupation of the house if it is a warehouse, a shop, or other place of business".

So, the question in any case is whether the servient owner's building retains sufficient light according to the ordinary notions of mankind for comfortable use and enjoyment. That is not to say that the amount of light to which the dominant owner is entitled will always be the same. If the nature of the building and its use for 20 years is such that it requires a high level of light, such as the greenhouse in *Allen v Greenwood*, then the measure of sufficient light reflects that.

As the right is a right to light to a particular aperture or particular apertures, if the dominant owner with a right to light changes their building to alter the position of the windows, the new windows will not benefit from the right to light that the old windows had. That said, if new windows are added which do not have a right to light and old windows with a right to light are unlawfully obstructed by an obstruction which also obscures the new windows, damages are recoverable for the obstruction to both old and new windows; see *Re London, Tilbury &*

Southend Ry and the Trustees of the Gower's Walk Schools (1889) 24 QBD 326.

The conventional method used by right to light surveyors to assess whether there has been an infringement of a right to light is to measure the amount of direct sky which will reach a hypothetical table 2 feet 9 inches high in the room behind the aperture in question. If despite the obstruction 50 per cent or more of the room's area receives at least one lumen of light at the level of such a table, it is regarded as adequately lit. This method was devised by a surveyor named Percy Waldram in the 1920s and the light contour diagrams produced using it are known as Waldram diagrams. It is not, however, conclusive. The Court can form its own view whether the room has been left with sufficient light and take into account the locality of the building and the higher standard of lighting expected nowadays; see *Ough v King* [1967] 1 WLR 1547. In *Beaumont Business Centres v Florala Properties* [2020] EWHC 550 (Ch) the Waldram diagrams were described as "only a starting point" (on the facts of that case).

If there is a building which has not yet acquired a prescriptive right to light because it or the windows in question have not existed for 20 years, it is possible for a neighbouring owner keen to prevent the right accruing to stop it doing so by obstructing the windows for at least a year. And rather than do that by erecting a screen, the neighbour can register a notice under the Rights of Light Act 1959 as a local land charge. The notice operates as a notional obstruction.

Where there is an existing right to light, an injunction can be obtained to prevent a building being erected which interferes with the right, or even in some cases to have the infringing building pulled down. For examples of injunctions being ordered to cut back buildings erected in breach of rights to light, see *Midtown Ltd v City of London Real Property Co Ltd* [2005] EWHC 33, [2005] 1 EGLR 65 and the *Beaumont Business Centres* case. If damages are awarded in lieu of an injunction the usual measure of damages is the amount that the parties might have agreed on as a fee to be paid to the dominant owner to allow the interference with their right to light in a hypothetical negotiation.

7. Conclusion

If a development of airspace above or subsoil below is being contemplated, it should be born in mind that the airspace may be affected by rights of light, or occasionally air, in favour of neighbouring owners; and subsoil may be affected by easements of support or other easements such as the right to retain pipes or cables running through it.

CHAPTER FIVE

LEASEHOLD ENFRANCHISEMENT AND STATUTORY RIGHTS OF FIRST REFUSAL

1. Leasehold Enfranchisement

The collective enfranchisement provisions in the Leasehold Reform, Housing and Urban Development Act 1993 ("the 1993 Act") give long-lessees of flats the right to have the freehold of the building containing their flats acquired by a 'nominee purchaser' (usually a company set up by the lessees for that purpose). The Leasehold Reform Act 1967 ("the 1967 Act") gives lessees of houses the right to acquire the freehold of the house demised to them. This section of this chapter is concerned with the question of how rights under the 1993 Act and the 1967 Act might impact airspace or subsoil separately from the building the freehold of which is being acquired.

In addition to the right to acquire the freehold, both the 1993 Act and the 1967 Act give lessees of the premises to which they apply the right to acquire a new lease by way of lease extension. That right to a new lease does not raise any issues that require discussion in this book as its exercise will enlarge the term of the existing lease without affecting the extent of the demised premises.

<u>The Leasehold Reform, Housing and Urban Development Act 1993</u>

The following paragraphs contain a brief summary of the collective enfranchisement process by way of introduction to the real topic of this chapter – enfranchisement as it impacts on airspace and subsoil. For a detailed discussion of all aspects of what is a technical area of the law replete with traps for the unwary, reference should be made to a specialist text such as Hague on Leasehold Enfranchisement (Sweet & Maxwell).

The right to collective enfranchisement under the 1993 Act applies to a "self-contained building or part of a building", containing two or more flats where the total number of flats held by "qualifying tenants" is at least two thirds of the total number of flats in the building or part-building to be acquired ("the premises") [ss. 1, 3]. The right extends to the freehold of the building itself and also to the freehold of any property outside the building which is appurtenant property demised by the lease of a qualifying tenant or which a qualifying tenant is entitled to use in common with occupiers of other premises [s. 1(2)(a)].

Where a new building or new storey is not yet fully constructed, the question may arise at what point it contains 'flats' for the purposes of the 1993 Act. In *Aldford House Freehold Ltd v Grosvenor (Mayfair) Estate* [2019] EWCA Civ 1848, [2020] Ch 270 the Court of Appeal held that a set of premises would not qualify as a 'flat' for the purposes the 1993 Act unless at some stage in its history it had reached a stage of construction to be suitable for use for the purposes of a dwelling.

Notice of the claim to enfranchise ("an initial notice") must be given by tenants of at least half the flats contained in the premises [s. 13(2)(b)]. The notice will specify a nominee purchaser which is to acquire the freehold, usually a company set up by the tenants for that purpose.

Where the premises are subject to other leases such as a headlease or a lease of the common parts of the premises, the lessees may be entitled or obliged to acquire the lessee's interest under that lease as well as the freehold [s. 2]. On receipt of notice of the claim, the freeholder of the premises responds by a counter-notice [s. 21] which must either admit or not-admit the claim. A counter-notice admitting the claim must state which proposals contained in the initial notice are accepted and make counter-proposals in relation to those which are not. If the freeholder proposes that any parts of the premises (other than the participating lessees' flats) be leased back to the freeholder, the counter-notice must say so. The right (and in some cases obligation) for the freeholder to have parts of the premises leased back are contained in s. 36 and Sch. 9 of the 1993 Act and applies to (a) flats not let to qualifying tenants (i.e. not on long leases), (b) commercial units and (c) flats let on secure or introductory tenants and some other housing association tenancies.

The right to collective enfranchisement does not extent to minerals underlying the building that the enfranchisement relates to *if* the owner of the minerals (usually the freeholder) requires them to be excepted and proper provision is made for support of the building [s. 1(6)].

Issues concerning airspace and subsoil are most likely to be raised by a lessees' claim to acquire the tenant's interest under an airspace or subsoil lease previously granted by the freeholder or a proposal by the freeholder for a leaseback of a unit including airspace or subsoil (such as a lease of part of the roof and the airspace above it to a mobile phone operator for the stationing of telecoms equipment). Otherwise, the freehold of the airspace above and subsoil below the premises subject to the collective enfranchisement claim is likely to go with the premises in the ordinary way in which it would do on a voluntary sale of the freehold.

In *LM Homes Ltd v Queen Court Freehold Company Ltd* [2020] EWCA Civ 371, [2020] QB 890, the Court of Appeal considered a claim for collective enfranchisement of a block of flats which was subject to (1) a lease of the surface of the roof and airspace above the roof, (2) a lease of a part of the basement situated below some of the block and (3) a lease of the subsoil below the block. All were granted with a view to developing above and/or below the building in due course. The lessees sought for the nominee purchaser to acquire the tenant's interests under those leases as part of the collective enfranchisement, a claim which was resisted by the respective tenants under the airspace and subsoil leases.

By s. 2 of the 1993 Act, the nominee purchaser would be entitled to the tenant's interests under the airspace, subsoil and basement leases if (1) the premises demised by those leases were common parts of the premises to which the Act applied and (2) the acquisition of the interests were reasonably necessary for the proper management or maintenance of those common parts, or (as the case may be) that property, on behalf of the tenants

Before the First-tier Tribunal (Property Chamber) and on an appeal to the Upper Tribunal (Lands Chamber) it was held that the nominee purchaser was entitled to acquire all three of the above leases. An appeal from the Upper Tribunal to the Court of Appeal was dismissed albeit that the reasoning of the Court of Appeal was not identical to that of the Upper Tribunal. In the Court of Appeal, it was held that:

1. The qualifying tenants were entitled to acquire the freehold of the airspace above and basement and subsoil below the block because of the principles (discussed in chapter 1 above) that freehold ownership of the surface and buildings on the surface will, as a general rule, carry with it the airspace above the building and subsoil below it. The ordinary principles of the common law apply to the qualifying tenants' right to have the freehold of a building to which the 1993 Act applies.

2. Furthermore, the tenants were entitled to the freehold of the basement as it was within the built envelope of the block.

3. The airspace, subsoil and basement were all parts of the 'building' to which the 1993 Act applies, for the purposes of sections 1 and 3 of the Act.

4. The airspace and subsoil came within the term 'common parts' for the purposes of s. 2 of the Act (as did the basement on the facts of the case). They did not cease to be common parts because leases were granted over them.

5. It was reasonably necessary for the nominee purchaser to acquire the tenants' interests under the airspace, subsoil and basement leases so that they would remain common pats within the control of the qualifying tenants.

6. It was also reasonably necessary to acquire the subsoil as otherwise the part of the subsoil demised by the subsoil lease might be developed by the lessee and then its function in supporting the building would change (even though the stratum of subsoil below the stratum demised by the subsoil lease would support the building instead).

7. It was reasonably necessary for the tenants to acquire the lessee's interest under the airspace lease because the airspace provides access to the roof which is required when maintenance of the roof is necessary and if the airspace were developed into flats that access would be lost.

Although the Court was dealing with the particular premises and particular airspace and subsoil leases in issue in the case, the approach taken is likely to be applicable to most leases of airspace above or subsoil below a building which is subject to a collective enfranchisement claim. The decision in *LM Homes* has the potential to be a real obstacle to airspace or subsoil developments over or under blocks of flats against the will of existing lessees.

Similar considerations were raised in *Merie Bin Mahfouz Company (UK) Ltd v Barrie House (Freehold) Ltd* [2014] UKUT 0390 (LC) but in that case it was the freeholder's claim to leasebacks of parts of the premises including airspace that was in issue. Two telecoms companies, Orange and O2, had leases of areas that included part of the surface of and airspace above the roof of the building which was subject to the collective enfranchisement claim, as well as rooms within the basement. The freeholder sought leasebacks of the premises demised to Orange and O2, subject to those companies' leases. The freeholder could only obtain leasebacks if the premises demised to Orange and O2 were 'units' defined as a separate set of premises let or intended for letting on a business lease which were contained in the building [s. 36, 38]. The tribunal held that the areas demised to Orange and O2 were units 'contained in' the building even though part of the units were aerials going into the airspace above the building. For the purposes of collective enfranchisement under the 1993 Act "the airspace immediately above the roof of a building can be regarded as being part of the building".

On the other hand, where there is an airspace lease for the purpose of development, the lessees seeking the freehold may not want to have to pay the premium required to acquire that lease. That was the position in *Hemphurst Ltd v Durrels House Ltd* [2011] UKUT 6 (LC), [2011] L & TR 16 where there was a lease of the whole roof and airspace above it and planning permission had been granted to build a penthouse flat on some of the roof. The lessees, presumably to reduce the amount they would otherwise have to pay, wanted to sever the lease into the part needed to build out the planning permission and the rest of the roof and airspace above it, and acquire only the rest. It was held that they were entitled to do so because once the penthouse was built it would only be reasonably necessary for them to manage or maintain the remaining part of the roof.

A further way in which this issue can arise is illustrated by *Vectis Property Company Ltd v Cambrai Court Management Company Ltd* [2022] UKUT 42 (LC). In that case, the question whether a development above a block of flats arose in the context of a dispute about the price to be paid for the freehold interest on a collective enfranchisement. There was no airspace lease but the landlord sought to include hope value of £203,000 in respect of the possibility of a development of the roof space in the amount payable for the freehold, whereas the tenants said that there was no hope value because a development was not possible. At first instance the First-tier Tribunal had allowed £25,000 for hope value on the basis that the development would not be possible without the lessees' agreement but held that £166,725 would have been payable as hope value if it was wrong about that. The freeholder appealed on the ground that £166,725 ought to have been allowed because it has a right to carry out the development; the tenants sought permission to cross-appeal on the ground that nothing should have been allowed. The Tribunal rejected a submission that *LM Homes* showed that a landlord cannot carry out a rooftop development which would make the existing roof inaccessible and difficult to maintain. The Tribunal held that that on the facts of the case there would be practical difficulties for a developer to address with carrying out a rooftop development but there was no legal impediment to doing so and so the hope value of £166,725 ought to be included in the amount payable for the freehold. The *Vectis* case is considered further in Chapter 9 below.

Basement level structures can also affect the question of what premises can be collectively enfranchised under the 1993 Act. As mentioned above, the premises that can be collectively enfranchised are a "self-contained building or part of a building", containing two or more flats. It will not always be obvious what constitutes a self-contained building for these purposes. It is not uncommon for a development to comprise a number of blocks of flats sitting on a single concrete slab, often with a basement car park situated below more than one of the blocks. Whether the blocks can be treated as one self-contained building will be a nuanced legal and engineering question. Whether all the blocks must be enfranchised together or individually will depend on the answer to that question. In *Consensus Business Group (Ground Rents) v Palgrave Gardens Freehold Co Ltd* [2020] EWHC 920 (Ch), [2020] 2 P & CR 13, a collective enfranchisement claim was made in respect of premises comprising five blocks of flats with an underground car park running underneath all the blocks and extending beyond the ground level footprint of the blocks. Falk J. held that the five blocks plus the car park made up a single self-contained building for the purposes of the 1993 Act, so that one collective enfranchisement claim could be made in relation to the whole of it. See also *Albion Residential Ltd v Albion Riverside Residents RTM Company Ltd* [2014] UKUT 0006 (LC) where it was held for similar reasons that the right to manage under the Commonhold and Leasehold Reform Act 2002 could not be exercised in relation to just one of two buildings both built over a car park and a single concrete slab.

The Leasehold Reform Act 1967

Under the 1967 Act, which applies to houses reasonably so called (a term which the Courts have struggled to define satisfactorily) issues regarding airspace or subsoil are less likely to arise. The right to enfranchise applies to "the house and premises" [s. 1(1)]. The premises for these purposes are any "garage, outhouse, garden, yard and appurtenances" which are let with the house and within its curtilage [s. 2(3)]. Airspace above and subsoil below a house will usually qualify as an appurtenance let with the house.

However, the lease of the house may be drafted so as to demise less than the whole house. If so, unless the part of the house not demised is so restricted as to be de minimis, the lease will fall outside the enfranchisement regime because it will not be of substantially the whole of the house. In *Field v Freehold Properties 250 Ltd* [2020] EWHC 792 (Ch), [2020] Ch 665 there was a lease of a house which expressly excluded all structural parts of the premises such as load bearing walls, roof and foundations. Marcus Smith J. held the freehold could not be acquired under the 1967 Act because the lease was not of substantially the whole house. During the course of his judgment he raised the possibility (but did not decide) that even a reservation of the airspace above the house from the lease might have that effect.

The 1967 Act also provided that the landlord can exclude underlying minerals from the conveyance of the freehold if they are included in the tenancy (there will be no right to enfranchise them anyhow if they are not included in the tenancy), so long as proper provision is made for support of the house [s. 2(6)].

2. Right of First Refusal Under Landlord and Tenant Act 1987

The grant of an airspace lease over a block of flats, with a view to development, raised similar issues under the Landlord and Tenant Act 1987 in *Dartmouth Court Blackheath Ltd v Berisworth Ltd* [2008] EWHC 350 (Ch), [2008] 2 P & CR 3 to those discussed above with reference to the 1993 Act. Part I of the 1987 Act, a notoriously badly drafted piece of legislation, gives lessees of flats a right of first refusal over disposals of (or out of) the reversionary interest in all or some of the building containing the flats.

The right of first refusal attaches to a disposal affecting any premises to which Part I of the 1987 Act applies. Subject to specified exceptions, a disposal is a disposal by the landlord of any estate or interest (whether legal or equitable) in the premises, including the disposal of an estate or interest in any common parts of the premises [S. 4(1)]. A disposal also includes a contract for or an assignment of rights under a contract for a disposal. So, the right of first refusal applies not just where the landlord of the flats in the premises is intending to sell its whole interest but also when it is proposing to sell or grant a lease of part of the premises, except for the grant of a tenancy of a single flat which is excluded from the right of first refusal or any of the other disposals excluded by s. 4(2).

Subject to exclusions for various categories of landlord, Part 1 of the 1987 Act applies to any premises which (a) consist of the whole or part of a building; and (b) contain two or more flats held by qualifying tenants when (c) the number of flats held by such tenants exceeds 50 per cent of the total number of flats in the premises [s. 1(2)]. A qualifying tenant is any tenancy except (a) a protected shorthold tenancy, (b) a business tenancy to which Part II of the Landlord and Tenant Act 1954 applies, (c) a tenancy terminable on the cessation of employment and (d) an assured tenancy or assured agricultural occupancy [S. 3(1)]. A person or company with tenancies of three or more flats in the premises is excluded from the definition of qualifying tenant. The rights granted by Part I of the 1987 Act can be exercised by the "requisite majority" of qualifying tenants which means more than 50% of the flats let to qualifying tenants [s. 18A]

Note that, as under the 1993 Act, a set of premises will not qualify as a flat for the purposes of the 1987 Act unless at some stage in its history it had reached a stage of construction to be suitable for use for the purposes of a dwelling (applying *Aldford House Freehold Ltd v Grosvenor (Mayfair) Estate* by analogy). So, flats sold off-plan before they have been constructed will probably not qualify as flats under the 1987 Act until they have reached a certain level of construction. That may be relevant to the point at which the 1987 Act begins to apply to the block of flats.

Where the right of first refusal exists, the landlord must serve a notice before making the disposal, or contracting to do so, giving the requisite majority of tenants the right to acquire the interest to be disposed of instead of the proposed purchaser or lessee. If the disposal is made, or an agreement to make it is executed, without the appropriate notice procedure having been followed, the requisite majority of tenants can acquire the interest in question from the purchaser or lessee.

Importantly for the purposes of this book, the right of first refusal may apply to a disposal of airspace or subsoil, such as the grant of a lease or an agreement to grant a lease of the airspace above a block of flats. It will apply if the airspace above the building (or subsoil beneath it as the case may be) is part of the "building" or "part of a building" which comprises the premises in question, or if is a "common part of the premises".

Dartmouth Court Blackheath Ltd v Berisworth [2008] EWHC 350 (Ch), [2008] 2 P & CR 3 concerned premises comprising a block of 72 flats with a garage block, paths and gardens. The freeholder granted a lease of the airspace above the roof of the block together with some other areas including basement rooms without first serving a notice under Part I of the 1987 Act. The tenants applied to the court for an order entitling them to acquire that lease. One of the issues that had to be determined by Warren J was whether the right of first refusal applied to the airspace above the roof. He held that it did on two alternative grounds. First, he held that the airspace above the roof at least up to the height of the chimneys was within the meaning of "building" as used in the Act because "it is an essential part of the space over which any owner of the Main Building with repairing obligations would need to have adequate rights of access". Secondly, he said that if his first ground was wrong the airspace was a common part as part of the exterior of the building. See also *York House (Chelsea) Ltd v Thompson* [2019] EWHC 2203 (Ch) in which Zacaroli J. followed Warren J. in *Berisworth*.

3. Conclusion

It appears from decisions made under both the Leasehold Reform and Urban Development Act 1993 and the Landlord and Tenant Act 1987 that a purposive interpretation will be given to those statutes to ensure that rights under them are not defeated by technical arguments as to whether airspace and subsoil are properly to be considered as part of a building to which either Act applies.

CHAPTER SIX

MINES, MINERALS AND MANORIAL RIGHTS

Mines and Minerals

1. Introduction

An exhaustive discussion of the law relating to mines and minerals is outside the scope of this work. The purpose of this chapter is to provide a brief summary of the law regarding ownership of mines and minerals and rights over them as part of the sub-soil of land, including manorial rights. Reference should be made to other sources such as Volume 76 of Halsbury's Laws of England for a fuller treatment of the subject covering such matters as the coal-mining industry (what is left of it) and statutory regulation of mines and quarries.

2. The Meaning of Mines and Minerals

There is no fixed, general definition of "minerals". In most contexts, whether a substance is a mineral is a question of fact having regard to what "minerals" meant to the mining world, the commercial world and among landowners at the time of the instrument in which the word is used; see *Glasgow Corpn v Farie* (1888) 13 App Cas 657. In *Coleman v Ibstock Brick* [2008] EWCA Civ 73 the Court of Appeal endorsed a summary of the principles relevant to reservations and exceptions of minerals given by Slade J. in *Earl of Lonsdale v Attorney-General* [1982] 1 WLR 887 which are as follows:

> "... (1) Unless the meaning is clear from the four corners of the relevant instrument itself, the first duty of the court in construing

a grant of mines and minerals is to try to ascertain what the phrase meant in the vernacular of "the mining world, the commercial world and landowners at the time of the grant": *Hext v. Gill*, L.R. 7 Ch.App. 699, 719, per James LJ, approved in *North British Rly Co v Budhill Coal and Sandstone Co* [1910] A.C. 116. (2) The meaning of the phrase in this vernacular sense may be derived either from direct evidence as to the vernacular meaning at the relevant time or by inference drawn by the court. (3) where it is clearly established that, at the date of the grant, a particular vernacular meaning was attributed to the phrase "mines and minerals" by "the mining world, the commercial world and landowners," the court will be predisposed to adopt that meaning, but the vernacular test is not a rigid test to be applied without regard to all the other terms of the instrument in question and the circumstances in which it is used. (4) The court must never overlook the commercial background and apparent commercial purpose of the transaction. (5) One pointer to the parties' intentions may be to consider whether or not the substances in question are exceptional in use, in value and in character: *Waring v. Foden* [1932] 1 Ch. 276, 294 per Lawrence L.J. (6) Another pointer is the evidence as to the general state of knowledge of the relevant substance at the date of the grant and the way in which it was then regarded and treated as a commercial matter. (7) A third, significant pointer may be derived from any express powers of working that are conferred by the instrument in question: ibid. (8) In considering whether a grant or reservation of mines and minerals includes a specified substance, it is irrelevant that the parties did not actually have that substance in mind. The test of their intention is an objective one."

There are, however, some statutes which expressly define the word. Substances that have been held to be minerals include basalt, brick-clay, china clay, terra cotta, copper, gravel, lead, limestone, marble, peat-earth, petroleum, stone, salt and sand. In different contexts, though, gravel, limestone, salt and sand have all been held not to be minerals.

Recently, in *Wynne-Finch v Natural Resources Body for Wales* [2020] EWHC 1924 (Ch), Falk J. had to decide whether Silurian mudstone, which makes up the subsoil of large tracts of land in rural northern Wales, was a mineral reserved by various nineteenth century enclosure awards and conveyances. She held that it could in principle be described as a mineral but on the facts was not within the relevant reservations of minerals. Her decision and the reasons for it were upheld by the Court of Appeal (*Wynne-Finch v Natural Resources Body for Wales* [2021] EWCA Civ 1473).

Similarly, the word "mine" does not have a fixed meaning; its meaning can vary according to the instrument in which it is used and the factual context. Originally it meant an underground excavation for the purpose of getting minerals; see *Glasgow Corpn v Farie*. But there can be opencast mines. The word "mine" is also sometimes used to mean a stratum of mineral, i.e. a vein or seam. And it can refer to the space where a mineral used to be before its excavation as well as the mineral itself. The word is expressly defined in some statutes such as the Coal Industry Act 1994.

3. Ownership

Mine and minerals (before their extraction) are part of the land and so presumed to be owned by the owner of the surface, subject to exceptions. As explained in chapter 1: there is a common law exception for gold and silver mines which belong to the Crown; by statute, unworked coal is vested in the Coal Authority and petroleum in its natural condition in strata beneath the surface vests in the Crown.

The presumption that mines and minerals are owned by the owners of the surface can be rebutted by showing that the two have been severed for example by a conveyance of the surface without mines beneath or of the mines alone. Evidence of long enjoyment of the mines separately from the surface is also capable of rebutting the presumption; see *Rowe v Grenfel* (1824) Ry & M 396.

There can be a right – a profit à prendre – to come onto another's land to extract minerals, which can be created expressly, by prescription, by custom or by statute, e.g. *Heath v Dane* [1905] 2 Ch 86.

In *ARC Aggregates Ltd v Branston Properties Ltd* [2020] EWHC 1976 (Ch), [2021] 2 P & CR 1 Zacaroli J. distinguished between an exception of mines and minerals from a transfer and a reservation of an incorporeal easement or profit in respect of them. Under the former, the transferor retains ownership ("the corporeal fee simple") of the strata below the surface but under the latter only a right to extract minerals is retained. He held as a matter of construction of the 1988 transfer before him, the transferor has retained ownership of the mines and minerals and not merely rights over them.

Although unlikely to be of importance nowadays, there is a principle that ownership of mines can be presumed from acts of ownership if there is not sufficient evidence to rebut the presumption; see *Ashton v Stock* (1877) 6 Ch D 719.

A consequence of the fact that mines and unworked minerals are part of the land is that statutory provisions relating to dispositions of land, and agreements to dispose of land, such as section 2 of the Law of Property (Miscellaneous Provisions) Act 1989 and sections 52-54 of the Law of Property Act 1925 apply to their sale and leasing. So, agreements to sell or lease must be made in writing, and contain all the terms agreed, and the transfer or lease must be made by deed (unless the lease is for under three years at the best rent reasonably obtainable). On the other hand, a contract to sell minerals to be obtained from a mine is a contract for the sale of chattels, not land. See also Ch.3, section 3 above on registration of interests in mines and minerals.

As mentioned in Chapter 5, the statutes providing for leasehold enfranchisement (the Leasehold Reform Act 1967 for houses and the Leasehold Reform, Housing and Urban Development Act 1993 for flats) both permit the landlord to retain the mines and minerals beneath the property being enfranchised, so long as provision is made for the support of that property.

4. Mining Leases

Since minerals are part of the land a lease can be granted of the minerals alone or the minerals with the surface, referred to as a mining lease. As the purpose of a mining lease is to extract and sell the subject matter of the lease, in some ways a mining lease is in reality a sale by periodic instalments in the form of rents or royalties.

As with all leases, it is important for a mining lease to describe the extent of the area demised unambiguously. Usually that is done with reference to the surface under which the minerals lie.

For obvious reasons, a lease of mines or minerals carries with it the right to extract the minerals (except coal, which vests in the Coal Authority) even if that is not made express. Normally there will be express powers to get out the minerals, though.

It does not follow from a right to work the minerals that there is a right to withdraw support from the surface. That right may be granted expressly in the lease. If it is not, it might arise by implication but only if an obligation not to let down the surface would be inconsistent with the terms of the lease; see *Butterknowle Colliery Co v Bishop Auckland Industrial Co-operative Co* [1906] AC 305.

5. Mining's Effects on the Surface

As discussed in section 3 of chapter 4, there is a natural right of support to the surface of land from strata below if they are in different ownership. That right can be modified, however, by the instrument conveying the mines or minerals separately from the surface or by some other instrument between the relevant parties, e.g. in *Sitwell v Earl of Londesborough* [1905] 1 Ch 460.

The modification may be express or by implication. So, if the surface is transferred without the mines underneath, or vice versa, a right to interfere with support for the surface might be implied if necessary to give business efficacy to the transfer. However, the absence of any provision in the transfer for compensation if subsidence is caused is likely to be inconsistent with any implied right to withdraw support; see *Butterknowle Colliery Co Ltd v Bishop Auckland Industrial Co-operative Co Ltd* [1906] AC 305.

As also discussed in chapter 4, while the natural right of support does not extend to buildings and other artificial structures, a right to support of artificial structures is an easement capable of being granted or reserved expressly or impliedly (an implied reservation of a right of support is far less usual than an implied grant) and capable of being acquired by prescription from long user. As an alternative to the grant or reservation of an easement of support, a restrictive covenant not to remove support from the surface, or an area of the surface may be included in a disposition of a mine or minerals.

The right of support does not entitle the owner of the surface to insist that minerals not be worked, but if they are worked adequate support for the surface must be provided (unless the right to support has been modified or given up or removed by statute); see *Harris v Ryding* (1839) 5 M & W 60.

On the other hand, it is possible in a disposition of minerals to specify that certain pillars not be worked, for example because they are supporting a building above.

The natural right of support may also be modified or removed by statute. For an example see the Mines (Working Facilities and Support) Act 1966, ss. 1 and 2(1)(a).

Damages for diminution in value and consequential loss are recoverable for infringement of a right of support, i.e. subsidence, caused by mining – both against the owner of the minerals and the person who caused the subsidence (if different). It is not necessary to prove negligence; see *Humphries v Brogden* (1850) 12 QB 739. That said, negligence may be relevant if the owner of the minerals relies on some statutory or other right to do the works which caused the subsidence. There may be a statutory remedy in place of the common law right to damages where the subsidence is caused by certain categories of underground workings, such as under the Coal Mining Subsidence Act 1991.

The surface owner will not necessarily be limited to a remedy in damages. An injunction to prevent further work may be available, and usually will be granted in a case of wrongful withdrawal of support, although the court has a discretion to grant damages in lieu of injunction in a suitable case; see *Coventry v Lawrence* [2014] UKSC 13, [2014] AC 822 for the most recent Supreme Court discussion of the discretion to grant damages in lieu of an injunction (discussed in Chapter 1 above).

Manorial Rights

6. Introduction

In some areas of England and Wales ownership of subsoil is complicated by a hangover from medieval times – the lord of the manor's rights to mines, minerals, limestone, lime, clay, stone, gravel, pits or quarries which survived the abolition of copyhold tenure by the Law of Property Act 1922. The issue is more common in some parts of the country than others, especially north-western England, because of the prevalence of copyhold tenure in those areas.

7. A Little Bit of Legal History

Until 1926, land in England and Wales could be held in two different ways: in freehold tenure (with which we are all familiar today, of course) and in copyhold tenure. Copyhold land was land that formerly had been held in unfree, villein tenure and so had been governed by the law of the manor (or rather manors, as each manor would have different customary laws). Ownership of copyhold land was, in effect, split between the lord and the tenant (the copyholder). Although many of the feudal aspects of copyhold tenure had fallen away by the end of the 16th century, the lord continued to have various rights over copyhold land, including ownership of timber growing on it and minerals under it. No new lordships of the manor could be created after the passing of the statute known as Quia Emptores 1290 and so each lord of the manor was the successor in title to the person who was lord of that manor in 1290.

Under manorial law, where land was copyhold the lord was entitled to the property in minerals under the ground but the tenant was entitled to possession of the minerals (except where the custom of the manor was that the lord was entitled to possession of the minerals too but that was unusual). So neither could mine the minerals without the agreement of the other. In *Eardley v Granville* (1876) 3 Ch D 826, Lord Jessel MR explained the position as follows:

> "The law seems to stand in this way: The estate of a copyholder in an ordinary copyhold (for it is an estate) is an estate in the soil throughout, except as regards for this purpose timber-trees and minerals. As regards the trees and minerals, the property remains in the lord, but, in the absence of custom, he cannot get either the one or the other, so that the minerals must remain unworked, and the trees must remain uncut. The possession is in the copyholder; the property is in the lord."

At common law, copyhold land could be converted into freehold land by the lord conveying to the copyholder the freehold of the land in question or by the lord releasing to the copyholder his "seigniorial rights".

Copyhold land was conveyed in a different way to freehold land, by "surrender and admittance", so it was impossible to convey freehold and copyhold land by the same conveyance. Due to that inconvenience and for other reasons, the Law of Property Act 1922 was passed to "enfranchise" (i.e. convert) all remaining copyhold land into freehold land. There had previously been three 19th century Copyhold Acts providing for voluntary enfranchisement. After the 1922 Act came into force on 1 January 1926 all land in England and Wales became held in freehold tenure.

The 1922 Act distinguished between three different categories of the lord's rights in land being enfranchised from copyhold into freehold. One category it abolished immediately. A second category of rights ("manorial incidents") was preserved until 1936. The Act made provision for manorial incidents to be extinguished by agreement or by following a statutory procedure. A payment to the lord to compensate for extinguishment of a manorial incident was required but if the voluntary or statutory procedure had not been followed by 31 December 1935, the rights were extinguished automatically.

A third category of right was preserved indefinitely and reserved to the lord despite the enfranchisement of all copyhold land, by s. 128(2) and Sch. 12, paras. 4 to 6 of the 1922 Act. Included in that category was any right of the lord in or to any mines, minerals, limestone, lime, clay, stone, gravel, pits or quarries in or under the enfranchised land; see para. 5 of Sch. 12 to the 1922 Act.

The nineteenth century Copyhold Acts providing for voluntary enfranchisement also excepted the lord's right to mines and minerals from the effect of enfranchisement unless there was agreement to the contrary.

The 1922 Act provided in s. 138(12) that the lord and the tenant of copyhold land could agree in writing to treat the lord's right to mines or minerals as a manorial incident and could extinguish it as if it were a manorial incident, i.e. by agreeing that the right be extinguished and agreeing the compensation for extinguishing it. S. 138(12) provided:

> "…where any such agreement relates to mines or minerals, the consideration for the estate or right shall be determined by agreement and not otherwise, and any such agreement for the extinguishment of the rights of the lord in or to any mines and

minerals shall, subject to the provisions of the agreement, operate as a conveyance to the tenant of such right notwithstanding that the agreement may not be under seal."

8. Manorial Rights to Mines and Minerals Today

The parts of the Law of Property Act 1922 dealing with copyhold land were repealed by the Statute Law (Repeals) Act 1969 on 1 January 1970. So, it seems that the procedure prescribed by s. 138(12) of the 1922 Act for extinguishment of the lord's rights to mines and minerals (agreeing to extinguish them as manorial incidents for compensation) may no longer be available. That Act has itself been repealed by a subsequent Act, but the repeal of a repealing statute by a subsequent statute does not revive a statute repealed by the first repealing statute unless words are added reviving it (and none were regarding the 1922 Act); see Interpretation Act 1978, s. 15.

Some statutory rights can survive the repeal of a statute pursuant to s. 16(1) of the Interpretation Act 1978. To survive, the right must be a "right, privilege, obligation or liability acquired, accrued or incurred under" the repealed Act before it was repealed.

Consequently,, the procedure laid down in s. 138(12) of the 1922 Act could only be relied on post-repeal if the mechanism under the Act for the lord and the tenant to agree upon the extinguishment of the lord's right to mines and minerals is a "right, privilege, obligation or liability acquired, accrued or incurred under" the 1922 Act at the date of its repeal.

It is questionable whether s. 16(1) would apply to an attempt to invoke the procedure under s. 138(12) after the repeal of the Act because it is doubtful that the ability to invoke that procedure amounts to a right or privilege for the purposes of s. 16(1) of the Interpretation Act. What is more, it is doubtful that s. 16(1) can apply when the parties to the agreement would not have been respectively the lord of the manor and the owner of the relevant land when the 1922 Act was repealed. The right or privilege preserved by s. 16 must have accrued or been acquired when the statute in question was repealed. Probably that means accrued to or been acquired by the party now seeking to exercise it.

Consequently, it is sensible to proceed on the cautious assumption that it is too late to invoke s. 138(12) of the 1922 Act in order to extinguish manorial rights to minerals by agreement. No alternative has been prescribed by statute. At common law, manorial rights in minerals were extinguished by a conveyance of the lord's interest in the minerals to the tenant. So, probably what is required now if a lord's mineral rights are to be extinguished by agreement is a deed by which the lord releases and assigns all interest the lord may have in minerals under the land to the freeholder.

There is some academic debate about the nature of the lord's right to minerals in copyhold land after it has been enfranchised. The Land Registry's view is that it is an incorporeal right, i.e. an interest in respect of land, rather than an estate in land. Hence it was an overriding interest and now can be protected by a notice rather than being one of the legal estates which must be substantively registered. Another view, put forward by some writers, is that the lord's surviving rights in formerly copyhold land, including his right to minerals, are an estate in land which ought to be capable of being substantively registered. For practical purposes, it is probably safe to adopt the Land Registry's approach. In *ARC Aggregates Ltd v Branston Properties Ltd*, the court accepted, without detailed discussion, that manorial mineral rights were an incorporeal right but did not find that of assistance when interpreting a 1988 transfer.

When unregistered freehold land or a registrable lease in unregistered land is first registered the freehold or leasehold estate vests in the registered proprietor subject only (so far as relevant) to interests which are the subject of an entry on the register or which override first registration under Sch. 1; see ss. 11(4) and 12(4) of the Land Registration Act 2002. Under the Land Registration Act 1925 and for the first 10 years of the life of the Land Registration Act 2002 manorial rights were overriding interests.

Manorial rights ceased to be overriding interests in registered land on 12 October 2013 by s. 117 of the Land Registration Act 2002. After that date a disposition (e.g. a sale, a charge, the grant of a lease) for value of registered land subject to manorial rights will take effect free of the manorial rights, by s. 29 of the Land Registration Act 2002, unless there is notice on the register protecting the priority of the manorial rights.

In the unlikely event that the manorial rights holder is in actual occupation of the land when an application is made for first registration, then the rights will often be an overriding interest by dint of the actual occupation under para. 2 of Sch. 1 to the Land Registration Act 2002, notwithstanding that manorial rights are no longer a separate category of overriding interest.

If the land subject to manorial rights remains unregistered, however, the registrar is required to make a note of the manorial rights on the register when the land comes to be first registered if the rights are protected by a caution against first registration or if the rights are revealed by the registrar's examination of the title. See rule 35 of the Land Registration Rules 2003.

The Land Registry maintains a searchable "index of relating franchises and manors" which contains details of registered lordship titles albeit the Land Registry does not maintain a definitive record of the extent of the original manor.

The sale of a manor carries with it the mines, minerals and quarries reputed or known as part, parcel or member of the manor; see s. 62(3) of the law of Property Act 1925.

9. Summary

Somewhat surprisingly, perhaps extraordinarily, the feudal form of land ownership known as copyhold survived until 1926 in some areas and even today there may be rights to mines and minerals held by the owner of a lordship under freehold land that prior to 1926 was copyhold. *Wynne-Finch v Natural Resources Body for Wales* was one such case.

When dealing with registered land, since 13 October 2013 the position has become fairly straightforward. Unless there is a note on the register to the effect that the land is subject to manorial rights (or unless the owner of the manorial rights is in actual occupation of the land), a purchaser, lessee or mortgagee will acquire the land, or their interest in it, free of any manorial rights to which the land may have been subject on registration of the transfer, charge or lease.

In relation to unregistered land, the position is more complex. If the land was formerly copyhold there is a possibility that ownership of the minerals under it vests in the owner of a lordship rather than the freeholder and a purchase or other disposition of unregistered land will not free it of manorial rights. That there is a claim to manorial rights to the minerals may be apparent from the entry of a caution against first registration asserting the rights. Even if there is no caution, if the land is believed to have been copyhold prior to 1926, a careful examination of the title documents is called for to rule out the possibility that the land is still subject to manorial rights.

CHAPTER SEVEN

FRACKING

1. Introduction

A fairly recent and controversial operation affecting subsoil is fracking, that is, extracting shale gas from shale rock formations by hydraulic fracturing. The process involves drilling a well to a depth of 1 to 5km and then injecting fluid into the rock deep beneath the surface to create small fractures in the rock. Gas that was trapped in the rock flows though the fractures into the well and up to the surface.

Fracking is commonplace in the United States but still a novelty in the UK. Whether its benefits outweigh its risks and disadvantages is a subject for another book but at the publication date of the first edition of this book the UK government was "encouraging safe and environmentally sound exploration to determine the potential" (Department for Business, Energy & Industrial Strategy Guidance on Fracking). So, a brief discussion of the property rights considerations around fracking was included in the first edition of this book. The present government does not permit fracking but policies change – the short-lived Liz Truss government intended to permit it. So the brief discussion of fracking in the first edition of this book is reproduced below in case it becomes relevant again.

2. Property Rights Considerations

Shale gas, like petroleum, is owned by the Crown but the subsoil strata containing it is not. That is owned by the owner of the surface above or, if legally severed from the surface, by the owner of the mineral rights in the subsoil containing the shale gas.

Consequently, a company wishing to conduct fracking operations will have to obtain rights from the owner of the surface where the drilling and associated operations are to take place, any separate owners of strata of subsoil beneath the surface, owners of neighbouring land under which horizontal drilling below the surface will take place (or owners of mineral rights under that neighbouring land), possibly other land needed to access the main land.

In order to facilitate the obtaining of such rights, the Infrastructure Act 2015, sections 43 to 49 provide a statutory right to use deep-level land for the purpose of exploiting petroleum, including shale gas or deep geothermal energy in England and Wales. Deep-level land is defined as being at least 300m below the surface. The Secretary of State can make regulations requiring operators to make payments where they exercise their statutory rights. The Act immunises landowners from liability in tort to others as a result of the exercise of rights under the Act, unless the damage is caused by a deliberate act or omission on the landowner's part.

Hence, the Infrastructure Act regime allows operators to avoid liability in trespass for deep-level incursions into land owned by parties unwilling voluntarily to grant a licence. As discussed in Chapter 1, *Bocardo SA v Star Energy UK Onshore Ltd* [2010] UKSC 35 established that it would be a trespass to drill without permission (statutory or otherwise) under land above "the point at which physical features such as pressure and temperature render the concept of the strata belonging to anybody so absurd as to be not worth arguing about".

Separately from the 2015 Act regime, the holder of a petroleum exploration and development licence (PEDL) granted by the Oil and Gas Authority on behalf of the Crown can obtain ancillary rights under section 7 of the Petroleum Act 1998 to overcome a landowner's unwillingness voluntarily to agree to drilling. Those rights include rights to enter, use and occupy land for laying and maintaining pipelines. The ancillary rights regime under the Petroleum Act (which incorporates the process to be followed under the Mines (Working Facilities and Support)

Act 1966) is cumbersome, hence the introduction of the less restrictive regime contained in the Infrastructure Act 2015, sections 43 to 49.

Of course, a fracking operator will also have to overcome other hurdles such as obtaining planning consent, obtaining rights of way and easements for services over neighbouring land, etc.

CHAPTER EIGHT

ADVERSE POSSESSION

1. Introduction

The reader will know that it is possible to acquire ownership of another's land by going into unlicensed possession of it (i.e. squatting on it) for sufficient years. For unregistered land, what is required is a continuous period of 12 years of adverse possession; see the Limitation Act 1980, s. 15 and Sch. 1[3]. For registered land, a period of 12 years of adverse possession that was complete by 13 October 2003 (the commencement date of the Land Registration Act 2002) will suffice; see Land Registration Act 2002, Sch. 12, para. 18. Otherwise, a period of 10 years' adverse possession of registered land is necessary, albeit not usually sufficient on its own, under Sch. 6 of the Land Registration Act 2002.

As about 85% of land in England and Wales is registered, and proving 12 years of adverse possession ending by October 2003 becomes harder with every passing year, most adverse possession claims nowadays are made under Sch. 6 of the 2002 Act. Under Sch. 6, the claim has to be made by way of an application to the Land Registry; see *Swan Housing Association v Gill* [2012] EWHC 3129 (QB), [2013] 1 WLR 1253. The 10 year period must continue until the application is made but a person who had been in adverse possession for at least 10 years until being evicted from the land (otherwise than by a court order) has six months from the date of eviction in which to apply (see para. 1 of Sch. 6). If the registrar is satisfied that the applicant has shown a prima facie case of 10 years of adverse possession the Land Registry will serve notice on the registered proprietor of the land. If the registered proprietor does nothing in response to the notice, the applicant will be registered as proprietor of

---

[3] The period in relation to Crown lands is 30 years.

the land. But if the registered proprietor responds he/she can (1) object to the application on the ground that in fact there has not been 10 years of adverse possession and/or (2) require the application to be dealt with under para. 5 of Sch. 6.

If the registered proprietor requires the application to be dealt with under para. 5, it will be rejected unless the applicant can satisfy one of the three conditions set out in para. 5, namely:

1. it would be unconscionable to dispossess the applicant because of an equitable (aka proprietary) estoppel,

2. the Applicant is entitled to be registered as the proprietor for some other reason (i.e. some reason in addition to his/her adverse possession of the land), or

3. the land claimed is adjacent to land belonging to the applicant and the applicant reasonably believed that the land to which the application relates belonged to him for at least 10 years of the period of adverse possession ending on the date of the application (under this condition there are 2 other criteria: (i) there must not be a determined boundary between the two plots, (ii) the land which is the subject of the application must have been registered for at least a year at the date of the application).

Disputes about whether the applicant can satisfy one of the para. 5 conditions, or was in fact not in adverse possession for 10 years or more, are referred by the Land Registry to be determined by the First-tier Tribunal (Property Chamber, Land Registration).

While a claim to adverse possession under Sch. 6 has to be made to the Land Registry, Sch. 6 can also be relied on as a defence to a possession claim brought in court if (1) there has been at least 10 years of adverse possession continuing until the bringing of the claim and (2) the third condition in para. 5 is satisfied. See s. 98 of the Land Registration Act 2002.

Adverse possession for these purposes requires proof of two things: (1) factual possession of the land by the squatter and (2) an intention to possess it (an animus possidendi as it was called in Law Latin). What is required for factual possession is that the paper owner has been dispossessed or has given up possession and the squatter has taken possession of the land. Possession for these purposes means exclusive possession, and not by the permission of the owner. It involves an appropriate degree of control of the land and dealing with the land in question as an occupying owner might have been expected to deal with it in circumstances where nobody else is dealing with it in that way. It is usual to infer the necessary intention where factual possession is shown. Reference should be made to *J A Pye (Oxford) Ltd v Graham* [2002] UKHL 30; [2003] 1 AC 419 for an authoritative statement of the law in this regard.

2. Adverse Possession of Subsoil

It is long-established that adverse possession can be taken of a stratum below the surface even though the paper title holder's ownership of the surface is not affected. In *Rains v Buxton* (1880) 14 Ch D 537 the plaintiffs had been in possession of a cellar beneath the defendants' land for over 60 years. Fry J held that the plaintiffs had obtained ownership of the cellar (but not the land above it) under the Real Property Limitation Act 1835.

The converse of a claim to adverse possession of a sub-stratum without the surface is a claim to adverse possession of the surface without a sub-stratum. In *Midland Railway Co. v Wright* [1901] Ch 738 a railway company owned land under which it built and used a railway tunnel. The defendant took possession of the surface of the land and remained in possession for long enough to establish ownership by adverse possession. It was argued that because the railway company had retained possession of the tunnel, the defendant could not have obtained title by adverse possession to the land on the surface. That was rejected by Byrne J who held that the defendant had acquired the surface of the land, with so much of what was beneath as was necessary for the enjoyment of it, subject to the right of the railway company to the tunnel and to so much of the strata beneath and above the tunnel as was necessary for enjoyment of the tunnel. He did not consider it necessary to identify the exact level under the surface at which the defendant's ownership stopped and the railway company's property began.

Much more recently, adverse possession of subsoil was successfully asserted in *Wynne-Finch v Natural Resources Body for Wales*, discussed above. In that case the dispute concerned ownership of mudstone beneath the surface of land in Wales. The surface belonged to the Defendant. The Claimants asserted ownership of the mudstone pursuant to manorial rights to minerals that they had acquired. The Defendant disputed that the Claimants or their predecessors in title had acquired title to the mudstone at all but in the alternative asserted that it had acquired title to the mudstone by adverse possession. At first instance ([2020] EWHC 1924 (Ch)), Falk J. found for the Defendant on both grounds. Insofar as adverse possession went, she held that the Defendant's actions in cutting into the ground to create roads or tracks and quarrying in some parts of the land were sufficient acts of factual possession and manifested an intention to possess the whole area in question. The Court of Appeal ([2021] EWCA Civ 1473) upheld the trial Judge's finding that the mudstone was not within the mineral rights acquired by the Claimants and so did not need to decide whether she was right on adverse possession Henderson LJ described the adverse possession issues as "both complex and difficult" and said it would not be appropriate to rule on them when it was not necessary to do so in order to dispose of the appeal.

3. Adverse Possession of Airspace

In principle, what goes for strata below the surface ought to go for strata above the surface. That is, it ought to be possible to obtain adverse possession of a layer of airspace above the surface (or a floor in a building) without obtaining possession of the surface itself. In *Stadium Capital Holdings v St Marylebone Properties Co Plc* [2009] EWHC 2942, that issue arose. An advertising hoarding on the wall of land belonging to the defendant projected over the claimant's land. The claimant sued the defendant for trespass. One of the defences raised by the defendant was that the defendant had acquired title to the airspace occupied by the advertising hoarding by adverse possession. The trial judge, Sir Donald Rattee, commented (at para.26):

> "It seems doubtful where the title to an area of air space not contiguous to the land underneath it can exist as a matter of law as an interest in land. It seems to me that the owner of land in respect of the air space above the land exist as an incident of the ownership of the land. Ownership of air space separate from ownership of the land underneath seems to be a very strange concept."

He did not decide the point of principle, however, rejecting the defendant's adverse possession argument for different (and better) reasons. It is respectfully suggested that the Judge's doubts were unwarranted. It is well established that an area of air space not contiguous to the land beneath can exist as a separate interest in land – that is exactly what a flying freehold is. And if it is possible to acquire by adverse possession a strata below the surface without acquiring the surface, as *Rains v Buxton* shows, there can be no principled reason why a strata above the surface should not equally be capable of acquisition by adverse possession separately from the surface.

An example of a case in which adverse possession was awarded of the surface but not all that was above it is *Williams v Usherwood* (1983) 45 P & CR 235, CA. In that case the defendants contended that they had acquired adverse possession of a strip of land that abutted the plaintiffs' house. The plaintiffs' eaves overhung the strip of land and their drains ran under it. The Court of Appeal held that the defendants had acquired the strip of land by adverse possession but "(a) without dispossessing the plaintiffs of the eaves or other projections or fixtures of or on their house and (b) subject to a right in the nature of an easement for the plaintiffs and their successors in title to enter on the [strip of land]… for the purpose of maintenance of the south side of [the plaintiffs' house], its windows and fixtures and its drainage apparatus." Hence, the Court of Appeal recognised that there could be adverse possession of some but not all of the airspace above a strip of land.

In conclusion, there is no reason in principle why a stratum below the surface or an area above the surface should not be acquired by adverse possession, albeit that cases in which a claim succeeds to adverse possession of an area below the surface or above the surface without the surface itself are likely to be rare.

CHAPTER NINE

BUILDING ABOVE AND BELOW EXISTING BUILDINGS

1. Introduction

In these days of housing shortage, it is increasingly common for freeholders to wish to erect a further storey or storeys of flats above an existing block. Basement developments below houses are also becoming commonplace in areas where property values are high enough to justify the expenditure. Apart from the obvious need to obtain planning permission and buildings regulations approval for such a development, particular thought needs to be given to the property and landlord and tenant implications. This chapter discusses some of those implications.

2. Who Owns the Airspace? Who Owns the Roof?

An obvious starting point when contemplating adding a storey to a block of flats is whether some or all of the present roof of the block, with or without the airspace above, is demised by any of the existing leases. If any of the roof and/or airspace on which the development is to take place is already demised, the development will not be able to go ahead unless the lessee(s) is/are willing to surrender the demised part of the roof back to the freeholder, doubtless for a premium. Reference should be made to Chapter 2 for a discussion of whether, and when, leases of top floor flats include the roof or roof and airspace above. It would be more usual in the case of a purpose-built block of flats for ownership of the roof to be retained by the landlord.

If there is a headlease of the whole block, two questions arise. Can the headlessee develop above the block? Can the freeholder develop above the block despite the headlease? The answer to both questions will turn, at least in part, on whether the airspace above the block is demised with the block. As discussed in Chapter 2, it is more likely that a lessee of an entire building will have the airspace above it included in its demise than a lessee of a flat or storey within the building.

3. Who Owns the Subsoil?

Most basement developments take place beneath freehold houses where there is no question that the freeholder of the house owns all the subsoil beneath (assuming no manorial rights or reservation of mines and minerals – see Chapter 6). In such a case, the main obstacle to development is likely to be the need for planning permission and compliance with the Party Wall etc Act 1996, rather than anyone else's rights over the subsoil beneath the existing building.

Should the house be leasehold, the question whether the subsoil is demised with it will arise. Again, reference should be made to Chapter 2. It is more likely that a lessee of the whole house, or the whole building in the case of a headlease of a block of flats, will have the subsoil beneath the flat included in their demise than a lessee of a ground (or basement) floor flat for the reasons discussed in that chapter.

4. Developments by Lessees

If it is a lessee that wishes to carry out the development (e.g. a headlessee of a block of flats or a lessee of a house), then, assuming that development might be possible because the airspace or subsoil (as the case may be) is within their demise, careful attention will have to be paid to the covenants in the lease restricting the lessee's rights to carry out alterations.

PRIOR CONSENT

Such restrictions may be absolute or may be subject to obtaining the lessor's prior consent. If the latter the covenant will usually provide that consent is not to be unreasonably refused, but if it does not do so a proviso against refusing consent to improvements unreasonably is to be read into the covenant pursuant to s. 19(2) of the Landlord and Tenant Act 1927 (so long as the covenant does not contain an absolute prohibition).

If the whole building is not within the demise of the lessee seeking to carry out the development, care will have to be taken not to infringe rights of support and/or protection from the demised premises to the rest of the building.

5. Landlords' Obligations Under Flat Leases

When it is the freeholder or a headlessee developing on top of a block of flats, an important consideration will be whether any of the landlord's obligations under the flat leases may be broken by the development – during the works to create it and/or when it is complete. The flat leases will contain express or implied covenants for quiet enjoyment, i.e. not to do anything that substantially interferes with the tenant's title to or possession of the flat or with his ordinary and lawful enjoyment of it. The landlord will also be subject to an implied obligation not to derogate from grant, that is not to use the land retained by him in such a way as to render the property demised by the flat lease unfit or materially less fit for the purpose for which the grant or demise was made. A thoughtlessly carried out rooftop development might be capable of infringing one or both of those obligations albeit that a rooftop development will not necessarily do so as a matter of course. In *Hannon v 169 Queen's Gate Ltd* [2000] 1 EGLR 40, a case concerning a flat tenant's attempt to prevent a rooftop development, the Judge, Bernard Livesey QC sitting as a High Court Judge, observed that:

> "...*prima facie* a landlord is entitled to use its retained property as it pleases, even where that will be detrimental to the interest of his

lessee: see *Port v Griffith [1938] 1 All ER 295*...Since it is accepted that the defendant's retained property includes the roof space and roof surface, it will have a *prima facie* entitlement to pursue the proposed development as planned."

In that case the Judge declined to imply a term into the flat lease that the landlord would not increase the number of flats in the building.

In *Vectis Property Co Ltd v Cambrai Court Management Co Ltd* [2022] UKUT 42 (LC), [2022] L & TR 22 (discussed in Chapter 8 above) the Upper Tribunal similarly held that a landlord of a block of flats had a right to build on the (not demised) roof of the building, without needing expressly to reserve the right to do so, as long as it did not interfere with the rights of others. The Tribunal held that the rooftop development contemplated in that case (creating two new flats on the roof) would not amount to a derogation from grant or breach of covenant of quiet enjoyment in itself, although if carried out carelessly it might do so.

In *Francia Properties v Aristou* [2017] L & TR 5, a county court judge held that by diminishing the amount of sunlight reaching the terrace of an existing flat a rooftop development was in principle capable of breaching the covenant for quiet enjoyment in the existing tenant's lease albeit that it would not cause a sufficient loss of sunlight to amount to a breach of the covenant in that particular case.

If the landlord retains the roof it will probably have repairing obligations in respect of it. In *Devonshire Reid Properties v Trenaman* [1997] 1 EGLR 45 it was held in the Lands Tribunal that a proposed rooftop development would involve the breach of that repairing obligation. In the *Hannon* case the Judge declined to follow *Trenaman* on that point, describing the principle behind it as "faintly absurd nowadays".

In the *Vectis Property* case, the Upper Tribunal held that the flat lessees' and management company's right of access to the roof of the building to repair it under the flat leases, and the management company's obligation to maintain the roof under the flat leases, were not legal impediments to developing on top of the roof. The Tribunal recognised, however, that there may be practical challenges in carrying out the development without infringing the access rights and preventing exercise of the repairing obligation in respect of the roof.

In *Lawson v Hartley-Brown* (1996) 71 P & CR 242, CA the defendant landlord built a two storey extension on top of the single storey retail premises let to the plaintiffs. It was held that the roof on which the construction took place was demised to the plaintiffs as part of their shop premises with the consequence that the development was a trespass. And because the lease demised the roof and there was no reservation of a right to build on it, the development was a derogation from grant. It was also held that the covenant for quiet enjoyment in the lease had been breached by the erection of scaffolding and the building work which interfered with the plaintiffs' enjoyment of their shop and the light to the shop windows. It may be possible to distinguish this decision in a case where the roof is not demised to any of the flat lessees and all reasonable steps are taken to minimise disruption during the building works.

The flat leases may contain a reservation of a right for the landlord to build on retained or adjoining property. If they do, the way in which that reserved right to build interacts with the tenant's right to quiet enjoyment and the landlord's obligation not to derogate from grant may depend on the exact wording of the various clauses. As a general proposition, however, it has been said that "the landlord's reservation of a right to build in a way which, but for that reservation, would constitute either a breach of the covenant for quiet enjoyment or a breach of the implied covenant not to derogate from the grant should be construed as entitling the landlord to do the work contemplated by the reservation provided that in doing that work the landlord has taken all reasonable steps to minimise the disturbance to the tenant caused thereby"; see *Timothy Taylor Ltd v Mayfair House Corp* [2016] 4 WLR 100 at [24]. Such a clause is unlikely to be construed in a way that deprives a right of the lessee under the lease, e.g. an access right, of any effect at all. There is an "irreducible minimum" of rights implicit in the obligation not to derogate from grant with which the express right to build is unlikely to permit interference; see *Petra Investments Ltd v Jeffrey Rogers Plc* [2000] L & TR 45.

6. Letting Schemes

In the *Treneman* case, the Tribunal accepted the lessees' argument that a term should be implied into the leases that the landlord would not create more than the 4 leases which were contemplated by the recitals of the 4 existing leases, and so could not add a new flat on top of the building. It was held that the four existing leases comprised a "letting scheme" of four flats and that the creation of a fifth flat would be inconsistent with that scheme. In the *Hannon* case the Judge accepted that there was a letting scheme but did not consider that it led to the conclusion that a term should be implied into the leases preventing the addition of more flats. A distinguishing factor was that in *Treneman* the recitals to the leases specifically referred to the intention to create 4 leases whereas the leases in *Hannon* did not mention a specific number of flats.

H Waites Ltd v Hambledon Court Ltd [2014] 1 EGLR 119 was concerned with a block of 12 flats and garages where there was a proposal to build new flats on the roofs of the garages. Morgan J. declined to imply a covenant into the existing leases that there should not be any additional flats created. He held that although there was a letting scheme for the estate, that did not support the implication of such a restriction because new flats would become subject to the scheme. The Upper Tribunal in the *Vectis Property* case followed Morgan J. in *H Waites* on this point, finding that there was a letting scheme in that case but that it did not prevent the creation of new flats on the roof.

7. Lessees' Easements

A further consideration will be the various easements – of way, for services, of support and protection, etc. – that the lessees are likely to have under their leases. If the development cannot be carried out without causing a substantial interference with any of those easements, the development will only be possible if an agreement can be reached with the relevant lessees.

8. Rights of Light

Depending upon the design of the existing building and the design of the proposed new storeys, the amount of light entering a window of an existing flat may be affected by the development. Under s. 3 of the Prescription Act 1832 a lessee can obtain a right to light against his own lessor after 20 years of uninterrupted enjoyment of light to the window in question. So, the design of the new storey will have to take into account its impact on light reaching existing windows in any building over 20 years old (a factor relevant to obtaining planning permission too). That said, a reservation of the landlord's right to build may operate as a consent and defeat a claim under the 1832 Act; see *Foster v Lyons & Co.* [1927] 1 Ch 219. Of course, rights to light of neighbouring buildings will have to be considered too.

9. Party Wall Etc Act 1996

If the development involves carrying out works to a 'party structure' as defined by s. 20 of the Party Wall etc. Act 1996 ("the PWA") notices under s. 2 of the PWA will have to be served on the relevant 'adjoining owner(s)' and party wall agreements entered into with them.

A party structure is defined by s. 20 as "a party wall and also a floor partition or other structure separating buildings or parts of buildings approached solely by separate staircases or separate entrances". A 'party wall' is defined as "(a) a wall which forms part of a building and stands on lands of different owners to a greater extent than the projection of any artificially formed support on which the wall rests; and (b) so much of a wall not being a wall referred to in paragraph (a) above as separates buildings belonging to different owners". So, where a rooftop development is contemplated it is likely that the lessees of top floor flats and possibly of all flats in the existing building would be adjoining owners for the purposes of the PWA.

Of course, there may also be works to a party wall between the building subject to the development and a neighbouring building which will necessitate service of s. 2 PWA notices on the neighbouring owner.

A basement development, or the strengthening of foundations to support the additional weight of a rooftop development may also trigger the need to serve notices under s. 6 of the PWA on neighbouring owners. The obligation to do so is triggered when there will be:

(1) excavations within a distance of three metres measured horizontally from any part of a building or structure of an adjoining owner and any part of the proposed excavation, building or structure will extend to a lower level than the level of the bottom of the foundations of the building or structure of the adjoining owner;

(2) excavations within a distance of six metres measured horizontally from any part of a building or structure of an adjoining owner and any part of the proposed excavation, building or structure will within those six metres meet a plane drawn downwards in the direction of the excavation, building or structure of the building owner at an angle of forty-five degrees to the horizontal from the line formed by the intersection of the plane of the level of the bottom of the foundations of the building or structure of the adjoining owner with the plane of the external face of the external wall of the building or structure of the adjoining owner.

10. Landlord and Tenant Act 1987

The existing lessees of a block of flats may have a right of first refusal under the Landlord and Tenant Act 1987 in relation to any proposed disposal by their landlord of anything other than a leasehold interest in a single flat. Disposals include the grant of a lease. So, a landlord intending to create, for example, an airspace lease to facilitate a rooftop development would be well-advised to take advice about whether it ought to first serve notices under the 1987 Act and whether the right of first refusal would apply to that lease. See *Dartmouth Court Blackheath Ltd v Berisworth Ltd* [2008] 2 P & CR 3 in which it was held that a lease of the airspace over the roof of a block of flats granted with a view to the creation of several new flats was a disposal to which the 1987 Act applied (discussed in Chapter 5 above).

11. Right to manage

Under Part 2 of the Commonhold and Leasehold Reform Act 2002 lessees of flats can acquire the right to manage their block of flats through a "right to manage" company (referred to as a RTM company). Where a RTM company acquires the right to manage a building under the 2002 Act, the landlord's management functions under the flat leases become functions of the RTM company (see s. 96 and 97 of the 2002 Act).

If a freeholder wishes to carry out a development on the roof of a block of flats where the right to manage has been acquired, the question will arise whether the RTM company's management functions are affected and if so whether that prevents the development. This issue was considered in the *Francia* case mentioned above where there was a RTM company in place. It was common ground in that case that the RTM company had management functions in respect of the roof (the Judge did not think it necessary to decide whether the management functions extended to the airspace above the roof). Nevertheless, the Judge held that the freeholder would be able to carry out a rooftop development providing that it had taken all reasonable steps to minimise the disturbance to the management functions of the RTM during and after the works. As the *Francia* decision was at county court level it did not create a precedent. However, the carefully reasoned conclusion on this point appears to be a sensible one.

12. Effect on Service Charges

Almost all leases of flats will include a provision for the lessee to pay a service charge. Some of them will stipulate that each flat should pay a "fair proportion" of the total cost incurred by the landlord providing services but often the lease will specify the proportion payable as percentage, based on either the number of flats or the floorspace occupied by each flat. Some leases which provide for a specified percentage will provide for the possibility of changing the percentage if the number of flats changes but many will not. What then happens if additional flats are added to the block? In the *Hambledon Court* case mentioned above the service charge percentage was specified, based on 12 flats. It was argued that because of that there should be implied a term that no additional flats could be created on the estate; but Morgan J held that a term that existing lessees should pay a fair proportion of the total instead of the specified percentage could be implied instead.

13. Highways

If a new construction will oversail the public highway, care must be taken not to infringe section 177 of the Highways Act 1980 which makes it a criminal offence to construct a building over any part of a highway maintainable at public expense, or alter a building so constructed, without a licence granted by the highway authority. A highway will include the pavement as well as the road itself, so a balcony overhanging the pavement, for example, would require a licence under this section.

It should be borne in mind that s. 177 does not apply to all public highways, only those maintainable at public expense (i.e. highways that have been adopted by the relevant highway authority). However, oversailing a roadway or footpath which has not been adopted would still be capable of being a trespass at common law (as to which, see chapter 1).

In *Build Hollywood Ltd v London Borough of Hackney* [2022] EWHC 2806 (Admin) it was held that s. 177 applied to wooden advertising hoardings attached to a building but projecting 20 cm over the pavement of a London road.

INDEX

A

Acquired right of support ... 41-42, 68

Adverse Possession ... 8, 81-86

Advertising ... 5, 17, 85, 96

Aircraft (see also, Drones) ... 4, 6, 46

Airspace ... 4-7, 10, 11, 12, 13, 17-21, 23, 27, 28, 33, 45-46, 53, 54, 55, 56, 57, 58, 60, 84, 87, 88

Ancient Lights ... 46, 47

B

Basement ... 22, 26, 53, 54, 55, 57, 60, 87, 88, 94

Boundaries ... 9, 28, 29

C

Cellar (see also basement) ... 9, 10, 14, 22, 23, 24, 27, 46, 83

CLM Handbook (see UK Finance Mortgage Lenders' Handbook for Conveyancers)

Coal Authority ... 3, 65, 67

Common law ... 1, 3, 4, 5, 8, 13, 38, 40, 44, 45, 46, 54, 65, 69, 70, 73, 97

Conveyancing ... 9, 29-31, 32

Copyhold ... 69, 70, 71, 72, 73, 75

Covenant ... 8, 19, 45, 68, 88, 89, 90, 91, 92

Crown ... 2, 3, 65, 77, 78, 81

D

Damages ... 6, 7, 39, 47, 48, 68, 69

Drainage ... 12, 13, 36, 43, 44, 86

Drones ... 5, 6

E

Easements ... 35, 36, 37, 38, 39, 41, 42, 43, 44, 45, 46, 66, 68, 92-93

F

Flats ... 18, 20, 21, 22, 24, 26, 27, 33, 34, 51, 52, 53, 57, 59, 60, 87, 88, 89, 90, 92, 94, 95, 96

Flight ... 4, 6, 7

Flying freehold ... 8, 9, 10, 11, 31, 85

Foundations ... 11, 13, 22, 23, 26, 58, 94

Fracking ... 77-79

Freehold ... 2, 7-11, 18, 28, 34, 51, 52, 53, 54, 56, 57, 58, 69-71, 87, 88, 89, 95

H

Highways ... 12-14, 44, 96-97

I

Injunction ... 5, 6, 7, 17, 48, 69

L

Land Registry ... 16, 27, 28, 73, 74, 81, 82

Landlord ... 19, 24, 56, 58-61, 66, 87, 89-92, 93, 95, 96

Law Commission ... 32

Leasehold ... 22, 23, 51, 52, 57-60, 66

Leasehold enfranchisement ... 51, 52, 66

Light ... 35, 36, 37, 38, 39, 46-49, 91, 93

M

Manorial Rights ... 69-75

Mineral Rights ... 73, 77, 78, 84

Minerals ... 3, 4, 8, 32, 53, 63-75, 84, 88

Mines ... 3, 7, 27, 32, 63-75, 78, 88

Mining lease ... 67

N

Natural gas ... 2, 44

Natural right of support ... See Support

Nuisance ... 4, 5, 6, 8, 45

O

Oil and Gas Authority ... 78

Ordnance Survey ... 9, 27, 28, 29

P

Petroleum ... 2, 3, 32, 64, 65, 77, 78

Pipes ... 2, 13, 42-44

Planning permission ... 56, 87, 88

Q

Quarries ... 69, 71, 74, 84

R

Right of first refusal ... 58-60, 95

Roof ... 8, 10, 17, 19, 20, 21, 22, 23, 26, 28, 53, 55, 56, 60, 87-88, 89, 90, 91, 95

S

Service Charges ... 96

Sewers ... 13, 42, 44

Shale Gas ... 77, 78

Subsidence ... 40, 68-69

Subsoil ... 2-4, 7-11, 12, 13, 14, 22-26, 27, 28, 29, 44, 51, 53, 54, 55, 77, 83-84, 88

Support ... 8, 9, 12, 13, 27, 36, 39-42, 53, 55, 58, 67, 68, 89

T

Telecoms ... 53, 55

Trespass ... 2-6, 17, 20, 30, 78, 85, 91, 97

U

UK Finance Mortgage Lenders' Handbook for Conveyancers ... 31

W

Water ... 36, 40, 42-45

MORE BOOKS BY LAW BRIEF PUBLISHING

A selection of our other titles available now:-

'A Practical Guide to Estate Administration and Crypto Assets' by Richard Marshall
'A Practical Guide to Managing GDPR Data Subject Access Requests – Second Edition' by Patrick O'Kane
'A Practical Guide to Parental Alienation in Private and Public Law Children Cases' by Sam King QC & Frankie Shama
'Contested Heritage – Removing Art from Land and Historic Buildings' by Richard Harwood QC, Catherine Dobson, David Sawtell
'The Limits of Separate Legal Personality: When Those Running a Company Can Be Held Personally Liable for Losses Caused to Third Parties Outside of the Company' by Dr Mike Wilkinson
'A Practical Guide to Transgender Law' by Robin Moira White & Nicola Newbegin
'A Practical Guide to 'Stranded Spouses' in Family Law' by Mani Singh Basi
'A Practical Guide to Residential Freehold Conveyancing' by Lorraine Richardson
'A Practical Guide to Pensions on Divorce for Lawyers' by Bryan Scant
'A Practical Guide to Challenging Sham Marriage Allegations in Immigration Law' by Priya Solanki
'A Practical Guide to Legal Rights in Scotland' by Sarah-Jane Macdonald
'A Practical Guide to New Build Conveyancing' by Paul Sams & Rebecca East
'A Practical Guide to Defending Barristers in Disciplinary Cases' by Marc Beaumont
'A Practical Guide to Inherited Wealth on Divorce' by Hayley Trim
'A Practical Guide to Practice Direction 12J and Domestic Abuse in Private Law Children Proceedings' by Rebecca Cross & Malvika Jaganmohan
'A Practical Guide to Confiscation and Restraint' by Narita Bahra QC, John Carl Townsend, David Winch
'A Practical Guide to the Law of Forests in Scotland' by Philip Buchan
'A Practical Guide to Health and Medical Cases in Immigration Law' by Rebecca Chapman & Miranda Butler

'A Practical Guide to Bad Character Evidence for Criminal Practitioners' by Aparna Rao
'A Practical Guide to Extradition Law post-Brexit' by Myles Grandison et al
'A Practical Guide to Hoarding and Mental Health for Housing Lawyers' by Rachel Coyle
'A Practical Guide to Psychiatric Claims in Personal Injury – 2nd Edition' by Liam Ryan
'Stephens on Contractual Indemnities' by Richard Stephens
'A Practical Guide to the EU Succession Regulation' by Richard Frimston
'A Practical Guide to Solicitor and Client Costs – 2nd Edition' by Robin Dunne
'Constructive Dismissal – Practice Pointers and Principles' by Benjimin Burgher
'A Practical Guide to Religion and Belief Discrimination Claims in the Workplace' by Kashif Ali
'A Practical Guide to the Law of Medical Treatment Decisions' by Ben Troke
'Fundamental Dishonesty and QOCS in Personal Injury Proceedings: Law and Practice' by Jake Rowley
'A Practical Guide to the Law in Relation to School Exclusions' by Charlotte Hadfield & Alice de Coverley
'A Practical Guide to Divorce for the Silver Separators' by Karin Walker
'The Right to be Forgotten – The Law and Practical Issues' by Melissa Stock
'A Practical Guide to Planning Law and Rights of Way in National Parks, the Broads and AONBs' by James Maurici QC, James Neill et al
'A Practical Guide to Election Law' by Tom Tabori
'A Practical Guide to the Law in Relation to Surrogacy' by Andrew Powell
'A Practical Guide to Claims Arising from Fatal Accidents – 2nd Edition' by James Patience
'A Practical Guide to the Ownership of Employee Inventions – From Entitlement to Compensation' by James Tumbridge & Ashley Roughton
'A Practical Guide to Asbestos Claims' by Jonathan Owen & Gareth McAloon
'A Practical Guide to Stamp Duty Land Tax in England and Northern Ireland' by Suzanne O'Hara
'A Practical Guide to the Law of Farming Partnerships' by Philip Whitcomb
'Covid-19, Homeworking and the Law – The Essential Guide to Employment and GDPR Issues' by Forbes Solicitors
'Covid-19 and Criminal Law – The Essential Guide' by Ramya Nagesh

'Covid-19 and Family Law in England and Wales – The Essential Guide' by Safda Mahmood
'A Practical Guide to the Law of Unlawful Eviction and Harassment – 2nd Edition' by Stephanie Lovegrove
'Covid-19, Brexit and the Law of Commercial Leases – The Essential Guide' by Mark Shelton
'A Practical Guide to Costs in Personal Injury Claims – 2nd Edition' by Matthew Hoe
'A Practical Guide to the General Data Protection Regulation (GDPR) – 2nd Edition' by Keith Markham
'Ellis on Credit Hire – Sixth Edition' by Aidan Ellis & Tim Kevan
'A Practical Guide to Working with Litigants in Person and McKenzie Friends in Family Cases' by Stuart Barlow
'Protecting Unregistered Brands: A Practical Guide to the Law of Passing Off' by Lorna Brazell
'A Practical Guide to Secondary Liability and Joint Enterprise Post-Jogee' by Joanne Cecil & James Mehigan
'A Practical Guide to the Pre-Action RTA Claims Protocol for Personal Injury Lawyers' by Antonia Ford
'A Practical Guide to Neighbour Disputes and the Law' by Alexander Walsh
'A Practical Guide to Forfeiture of Leases' by Mark Shelton
'A Practical Guide to Coercive Control for Legal Practitioners and Victims' by Rachel Horman
'Tackling Disclosure in the Criminal Courts – A Practitioner's Guide' by Narita Bahra QC & Don Ramble
'A Practical Guide to the Law of Driverless Cars – Second Edition' by Alex Glassbrook, Emma Northey & Scarlett Milligan
'A Practical Guide to TOLATA Claims' by Greg Williams
'A Practical Guide to Elderly Law – 2nd Edition' by Justin Patten
'A Practical Guide to Responding to Housing Disrepair and Unfitness Claims' by Iain Wightwick
'A Practical Guide to the Construction and Rectification of Wills and Trust Instruments' by Edward Hewitt
'A Practical Guide to the Law of Bullying and Harassment in the Workplace' by Philip Hyland

'How to Be a Freelance Solicitor: A Practical Guide to the SRA-Regulated Freelance Solicitor Model' by Paul Bennett
'A Practical Guide to Prison Injury Claims' by Malcolm Johnson
'A Practical Guide to the Small Claims Track – 2nd Edition' by Dominic Bright
'A Practical Guide to Advising Clients at the Police Station' by Colin Stephen McKeown-Beaumont
'A Practical Guide to Antisocial Behaviour Injunctions' by Iain Wightwick
'Practical Mediation: A Guide for Mediators, Advocates, Advisers, Lawyers, and Students in Civil, Commercial, Business, Property, Workplace, and Employment Cases' by Jonathan Dingle with John Sephton
'The Mini-Pupillage Workbook' by David Boyle
'A Practical Guide to Crofting Law' by Brian Inkster
'A Practical Guide to the Law of Domain Names and Cybersquatting' by Andrew Clemson
'A Practical Guide to the Law of Gender Pay Gap Reporting' by Harini Iyengar
'NHS Whistleblowing and the Law' by Joseph England
'Employment Law and the Gig Economy' by Nigel Mackay & Annie Powell
'A Practical Guide to Noise Induced Hearing Loss (NIHL) Claims' by Andrew Mckie, Ian Skeate, Gareth McAloon
'An Introduction to Beauty Negligence Claims – A Practical Guide for the Personal Injury Practitioner' by Greg Almond
'Intercompany Agreements for Transfer Pricing Compliance' by Paul Sutton
'Zen and the Art of Mediation' by Martin Plowman
'A Practical Guide to the SRA Principles, Individual and Law Firm Codes of Conduct 2019 – What Every Law Firm Needs to Know' by Paul Bennett
'A Practical Guide to Adoption for Family Lawyers' by Graham Pegg
'A Practical Guide to Industrial Disease Claims' by Andrew Mckie & Ian Skeate
'A Practical Guide to Redundancy' by Philip Hyland
'A Practical Guide to Vicarious Liability' by Mariel Irvine
'A Practical Guide to Applications for Landlord's Consent and Variation of Leases' by Mark Shelton
'A Practical Guide to Relief from Sanctions Post-Mitchell and Denton' by Peter Causton
'A Practical Guide to Equity Release for Advisors' by Paul Sams

'A Practical Guide to Financial Services Claims' by Chris Hegarty
'The Law of Houses in Multiple Occupation: A Practical Guide to HMO Proceedings' by Julian Hunt
'Occupiers, Highways and Defective Premises Claims: A Practical Guide Post-Jackson – 2nd Edition' by Andrew Mckie
'A Practical Guide to Financial Ombudsman Service Claims' by Adam Temple & Robert Scrivenor
'A Practical Guide to Running Housing Disrepair and Cavity Wall Claims: 2nd Edition' by Andrew Mckie & Ian Skeate
'A Practical Guide to Holiday Sickness Claims – 2nd Edition' by Andrew Mckie & Ian Skeate
'Arguments and Tactics for Personal Injury and Clinical Negligence Claims' by Dorian Williams
'A Practical Guide to Drone Law' by Rufus Ballaster, Andrew Firman, Eleanor Clot
'A Practical Guide to Compliance for Personal Injury Firms Working With Claims Management Companies' by Paul Bennett
'RTA Allegations of Fraud in a Post-Jackson Era: The Handbook – 2nd Edition' by Andrew Mckie
'RTA Personal Injury Claims: A Practical Guide Post-Jackson' by Andrew Mckie
'On Experts: CPR35 for Lawyers and Experts' by David Boyle
'An Introduction to Personal Injury Law' by David Boyle

These books and more are available to order online direct from the publisher at www.lawbriefpublishing.com, where you can also read free sample chapters. For any queries, contact us on 0844 587 2383 or mail@lawbriefpublishing.com.

Our books are also usually in stock at www.amazon.co.uk with free next day delivery for Prime members, and at good legal bookshops such as Wildy & Sons.

We are regularly launching new books in our series of practical day-to-day practitioners' guides. Visit our website and join our free newsletter to be kept informed and to receive special offers, free chapters, etc.

You can also follow us on Twitter at www.twitter.com/lawbriefpub.

Printed in Great Britain
by Amazon

59471417R00077